I063886 8

The Little Book

of

SCOTTISH

FOLKLORE

The Little Book
of
SCOTTISH
FOLKLORE

Retold by
Joules & Ken Taylor

SIENA

This edition published and distributed by Siena, 1999

Siena is an imprint of Parragon

Parragon
Queen Street House
4 Queen Street
Bath BA1 1HE

Produced by Magpie Books, an imprint of
Robinson Publishing Ltd, London

Cover illustration courtesy of The Bridgeman Art
Library

ISBN 0 75252 767 3

A copy of the British Library Cataloguing-in-
Publication Data is available from the British Library
Printed in China

Contents

~

Introduction

Scotland . . . Land of the brave. Land of mist-shrouded lochs and snow-clad mountains, ancient castles and mysterious glens: and home of the canny Scots, descendants of the ancient Pict and Celtic peoples, their hardy character sculpted by the wild and rugged landscape of their motherland. Dour, dryly humorous, inventive folk, and valiant warriors – so much so that the Romans had to build a mighty wall from coast to coast to keep them back!

In the words of the old traditional toast:

> Here's tae us!
> Who's like us?
> Damn few – and they're all dead!

THE FEY-FOLK

Scotland is rich in lore of the Fey-Folk —
supernatural beings, some benign, some
malevolent, but all of them magical and
possessed of mysterious powers.

Perhaps the most wonderful of the Fey-Folk
are the Seelie Court — the "Good People," "Fair
Folk" or "Blessed Host" — who form the fairy
aristocracy. These tall, graceful beings live in an
Otherworld, usually under lakes or in hollow
hills, where it is always summer and time passes
differently from the mortal world.

Sometimes they leave their magical realm to
visit the earthly world, riding forth at the ancient
festivals of May Day and Hallowe'en to bless the
crops of mortal men and perform small
kindnesses according to their whim. Their

counterpart is the Unseelie Court, a malevolent, vengeful band mostly made up of the souls of those who died unsanctified and now prey on the envied living.

The fairy peasantry, such as Brownies and trolls, are usually solitary, and small of stature, and sometimes helpful toward humans.

The seas around the craggy coasts house mermaids, selkies and roanes, and the glens and lochs are the haunts of strange and monstrous creatures.

The Orkney and Shetland islands were the strongholds of giants. And the country has had its fair share of witches, as well as one famous magician, Michael Scott, who, legend has it, lured the Plague to the Abbey at Glenluce and locked it in a vault . . .

Little Helper

Brownies can be very helpful, but they are also easily offended, and it's wise to be careful of what you say when they are near . . .

There was a Brownie who for many years threshed corn at Cranshaws farm, piling it into a neat stack, or "mow," in the barn with the grateful farmer thanking the Brownie with gifts of food and drink. All went well until someone commented, thoughtlessly, that the corn was not "well mowed."

The Brownie was furious!

"It's no' well mowed? It's no' well mowed? Then it'll ne'er be mowed by me again!"

He spent all the next night carrying the corn from the barn to a stream two miles away, where he tipped the whole lot into the water.

Needless to say, the Brownie was never seen again . . .

Tam Lin

Brave Janet, the daughter of a Scottish nobleman, went one summer afternoon to the well in the elf-guarded wood . . .

It was well known that no maiden returned from the wood unscathed, but Janet was heedless – and not a little curious – and she plucked a rose from the well's encircling briar. Immediately the Fairy Guardian appeared before her, a young knight, pale, comely and dressed in silk.

Janet lost her heart – and her maidenhood – to him, and, unlike the other young women, returned to the wood again and again. During the drowsy summer afternoons the knight revealed to her that he was as human as she, and had been stolen by the Fey-Folk as he lay unconscious after a fall from his horse many years before. Now, deeply in love with Janet, he wished to escape the fairies' power – but only with her help was this possible.

Heeding his advice, at Hallowe'en she waited at the crossroads in the woods until the Fey-Folk rode by, pale and beautiful and mounted on night-black horses. Janet leapt from her hiding place and pulled her lover from his white horse. She held him fast as the Queen first turned him into a huge, poisonous serpent, then a savage bear, then a hissing, writhing swan. Finally he became a red-hot bar of iron, and Janet, realizing this was the last transformation, ran to the well and dropped in the metal – whereupon Tam Lin arose in his own shape, freed from the Queen's bondage.

Powerless, the Queen could do nothing but bewail her loss. But Janet and her lover, together at last, scarcely heard . . .

Tam Lin

"Oh, I forbid you, maidens all,
Who are so sweet and fair,
To go down into Carterhaugh Wood,
For young Tam Lin is there . . ."

Then spoke the lady Janet fair,
Fairest of all her kin,
"I'll come and go there as I like –
Nor need ask leave of him!"

She dressed herself, and preened herself,
From her hair down to her toe,
Then she's off to speak with young Tam Lin
As fast as she can go.

He took her by her milk-white hand
And by her green silk sleeve,
And laid her low upon the flowers
And never asked her leave . . .

"One day as I rode to the hunt,
Dead sleep upon me fell,
The Queen of Faerie she was there
And took me to hersel'.

Now, Faerie is a pretty place
In which I love to dwell,
But at the end of seven years
The last there goes to hell –
And as a human being, I fear
the next will be mysel'...

At Hallowe'en, my Janet,
The Faerie Court will ride,
And if you have the courage,
You may yet become my bride.

Seize upon me with a spring
And pull me to the earth,
They'll shape me in your arms, my love,
'Til you be frit near death..."

She holds him through the changes,
Til human he was again,
And a cry went through the Faerie Court
That the maid had rescued her ain.

"Had I known" the Queen did say
"Before we came from home,
I'd have taken out your heart of flesh
And given you one of stone . . ."

The Seal-Folk

~

The seal-folk – selkies – are most often seen around the Orkney and Shetland islands, although they have been found on more southerly coasts of the mainland from time to time.

Like their cousins, the merfolk – with whom they coexist peacefully – they live mostly in the depths of the sea. But there the similarity ends.

Selkies wear the skins of seals when moving through the water: these soft, silky pelts protect them from harm and allow them to swim with great speed and grace through the ocean. On land, they remove the seal-skin and become almost indistinguishable from mortal humans, except for the webbed skin between their fingers and toes.

Both the men and the women are

possessed of a rare, almost unearthly beauty, causing many humans to desire them. Male selkies have often taken human lovers and produced offspring – always with webbed toes and fingers – but the females are shy and easily frightened, and can only be captured by the theft of their seal-skins, which forces them to remain on land.

This can be most easily accomplished while the selkie maidens are dancing on the seashore – something for which they have a passion. Any human bold enough to steal a selkie's skin may be rewarded by a faithful, beautiful mate for as long as he keeps the skin hidden. If the selkie can find her seal-skin, she will return immediately to the sea and never return, leaving her human lover to lament his fate.

It is vitally important that selkie blood never be allowed to drip into the sea, as this will produce violent storms in which even the sturdiest boats will be wrecked.

Weight-lifting Witches . . .

~

On the moor behind the ruins of Craig-
maddie Castle, to the north of Glasgow, is a
strange "arch" of boulders known as the Auld
Wives' Lichts . . .

Way back in the mists of time, three
sisters, witches of considerable renown,
challenged each other to a trial of strength.
The first, confident of her success, lifted a
huge boulder onto her shoulder, strode
across the moor, and dropped it on the
ground within a wide, shallow depression.

The second sister hauled a slightly larger
rock into her arms and staggered over to the
first boulder, where she lowered her own,
with a grunt and a groan, so that it stood
proud beside her sister's.

The third, eldest, witch sneered at her
siblings' efforts and hoisted a huge boulder,
ran across the moor with it balanced –

somewhat precariously, according to some legends – on her head, and lowered it resolutely to sit atop the other two . . .

There could be no argument that she had won the challenge, much to her sisters' annoyance. They conceded the contest – but not before laying a spell upon the archway they had created.

To this day the place has an eerie, almost frightening atmosphere. Even on the warmest day the immediate vicinity is supernaturally cold, raising gooseflesh on those who dare to approach.

Visitors have reported feeling as though they are being watched – and not by a friendly entity! And on occasion, particularly at Hallowe'en, and dark (new) moon, the stench of newly spilled blood fills the air . . .

Nevertheless, stalwart couples still crawl through the archway for luck – and usually get it, too. After all, "Who dares, wins . . ."

The Great Worms

~

Most countries have their legendary dragons, and Scotland is no exception. One such terrorized the land around Linton until it was slain, reputedly by John Somerville who, it is said, was later knighted by King William for the act.

The dragon had been attacking everything and everyone that came its way. Arrows had been ineffective, and no one had dared to approach close enough to use a sword or lance. John Somerville attached a small wheel soaked in pitch to the point of his lance, and when the dragon appeared, had his servant light the flammable tar: ramming the lance into the creature's throat he so severely wounded it that it died soon after. The impression of its coils can still be seen on the hillock where it writhed in agony as it died.

Another famous dragon lived near the well at the village of Pittempton, not far from Dundee. A farmer sent his eldest daughter to fetch water from the well; when she didn't return he sent her younger sister, then the next youngest, until all nine daughters had gone to the well and not returned.

Catching up his spear, the farmer went to the well and found a great dragon lying there, covered with the blood of his daughters. Unable to tackle the serpent by himself, he gathered the villagers and they gave chase.

The dragon tried to escape, but was finally cornered. Martin, the lover of one of the daughters, then killed the beast with his club. In memory of the event the spring was named, for a time, "Nine Maidens' Well."

The Demon Lover

"O wither hae ye been, my lang-lost love,
This lang seven years and more?"
"Now I've come back to claim the vows
Ye made to me before."

"O hold your tongue of those old vows
For I am become a wife,
O hold your tongue of those old vows
For I've given twa bairns life."

"O false are the vows o' womankind,
But fair is their false bodie,
I wouldna hae left, my fortune to find,
Had it no' been for love o' thee."

"Now see ye not yon seven great ships
The eighth brought me to land,
With merchandise and mariners
And wealth in ilka hand?"

Then she's gane to her twa wee bairns,
Kissed them baith on cheek and chin;
Sae has she to her sleeping husband
And bid the same farewell to him.

The masts o' the ship were beaten gold
And bent not wi' the heaving seas,
The sails were o' the finest silk
But filled not with the easterly breeze.

The hadna sailed a league, a league,
A league but barely three,
Until she spied his cloven hoof
And she wept right bitterly.

She cried "What pleasant hills are they
The sun shines sweetly on?"
"O yon are the hills o' heaven," he said,
"Where you will never win."

"O what sort o' mountain's yon?" she said,
"Sae dreary wi' frost and snow?"
"O yon is the mountain o' hell," he cried,
"Where you and I will go!"

And when she turned her round about,
Taller he seemed to be;
Until the tops o' that gallant ship
Nae taller were than he.

The clouds grew dark, the winds grew loud,
And the tears o'er filled her eye,
And awesome wailed the snow white sprites
Upon the foaming sea.

He struck the topmast wi' his hand,
The foremast wi' his knee;
And broke that great ship clear in twain,
And sank her in the sea.

Household Brownies

~

Brownies sometimes lived beneath the thresholds or hearths of human houses. The flat hearth stone or doorstep formed part of the roof of their own subterranean dwellings.

There was often great neighborliness between the little folk and the humans above, with the Brownies borrowing items – most often iron kettles or cauldrons – and later returning them filled with fine food and drink or even fairy gold. Favors done to them, sometimes as simple a thing as avoiding a pathway they particularly use, could be rewarded by prosperity and good health.

It was important to remain silent in such dealings with the little people, as speaking could break the charm and leave the human with nothing. Wise folk would also keep very quiet about their business with the Brownies, for fear of others finding out – and having the fairy gold turn into withered leaves.

On the other hand, hurting or offending them could have the opposite effect, bringing anything from minor inconveniences to major calamity on the family of anyone so foolish!

The Giants of the North

While a few were known on the mainland, most of Scotland's giants inhabited the Orkney and Shetland islands – which was lucky, because in general they were a troublesome lot, continually quarreling and throwing stones at each other, much to the dismay of the islanders!

Two giant brothers, Herman and Saxi, who lived on the Shetland island of Unst, both fell in love with the same mermaid. Being both a tease, and a little alarmed at being the object of affection of such a pair, she promised to marry the one who would follow her to the North Pole.

Both brothers leapt into the sea, and were never seen again. (Neither was the mermaid – we can only wonder if either giant succeeded in winning her!)

Sigger, another Unst giant, used to move

boulders around the island, creating obstacles for his human neighbors. He was eventually killed when a huge rock fell upon him. It is not known whether the islanders had anything to do with the accident . . .

Some giants, however, were less of a nuisance. Cubbie Roo, who lived on the Orkney island of Wyre, was renowned as a bridge-builder, and many of the rock stacks and islets around the island are held to be the foundations and pillars of his bridges. There is a tradition that his aim was to link all the islands by means of his bridges – a noble dream, but one he didn't live to accomplish.

A fellow of his on Rousay, possibly in search of a wife, kidnapped one by one the three daughters of his neighbor, a farmer, and set them to work milking his cows and preparing the fleece from his sheep in readiness for weaving.

The first two daughters failed in their

tasks: the giant expected the work done in an impossibly short space of time. The third, however, was a kind and charming girl, and a friend of the Fey-Folk, who helped her complete the work. Pleased by her industry, the giant treated her well, and even accompanied her two sisters back home – where her father killed him by upending a cauldron of boiling blood over his head!

In common with trolls, sunlight turned giants to stone, and most of them kept themselves hidden during the day. However, Menia and Fenia, sister giantesses, overcame this problem by living underwater in the Pentland Firth. They earned a living by grinding salt from the sea with an enchanted grindstone and selling it to their dry-land kin for food seasoning. When they were working, a whirlpool would appear in the Firth's surface.

The Kelpie

From their earliest days, in ancient times children were warned about the dangers of approaching stray horses near rivers . . .

The kelpie is a fabulous, immortal beast, in shape a glossy, noble stallion with an apparently placid nature. It haunts the banks of rivers and streams, cropping the sweet grass and giving every indication of tameness and gentle temperament. Indeed, it seems almost to invite the unwary traveler to ride awhile and rest his weary legs.

But should he mount the animal, it immediately snarls and rears and charges straight for the deepest part of the river, plunging in and rolling over and over until the human is drowned – whereupon the kelpie devours its newly dead prey!

Although a vicious and fearsome beast, the kelpie can be overcome. If a human succeeds in bridling the creature, it will be compelled to work for him – at least until it finds a way to remove the bridle. And since the kelpie's strength is prodigious, it is able to haul, alone and in an hour, loads that would normally take a team of heavy horses at least a day to shift.

Of course, forcing such a perilous creature to work for you is at best a risky business, and at worst can be deadly. At Morphie, not far from Montrose on the east coast, the laird had compelled a local kelpie to haul the stones for his castle. On completion of the building, when the creature was set free it cursed the laird, saying:

> "Sore back and sore bones
> Pulling the laird's stones!
> The laird'll never thrive
> While the kelpie is alive!"

Sure enough, his bloodline was soon extinct . . .

Annan Water

He rode that night both bold and bonnie
To pledge himself to marry Annie
But Annan flowed full haste in spate
And the ferryman sternly bade him wait.

But the fiery love that lighted his heart
Could no wise bear they wait apart
But stripped him o' his coat and shoon
And plunged him in the icy foam.

An easy ford in summer droughts
The raging winter torrent shouts
"Beware the Kelpie o' Annan
The doom o' sae many a man!"

Though he swam baith strang and steady
The far bank's briars gave him nae gangway.
And then above the roaring water
The Kelpie's shriek told of his slaughter!

The Three-headed Ogre of the Borders

~

On a hill at Duns stands the Celtic fort called
Edin's Hall Broch...

Red Etin was a fearsome figure, a giant
with three heads and a mighty appetite for
human flesh, whose constant search for food
was accompanied by his rumbling chant:

"Snouk butt, and snouk ben,
I smell the smell of a mortal man;
Be he living or be he dead,
His heart this night shall season my bread."

A poor widow's elder son went out into the
world to seek his fortune, leaving his younger
brother with a knife that would reflect his fate
– if it remained bright and sharp he was well,
but if it rusted, then ill would have befallen
him. Sure enough, he soon encountered Red
Etin, and, being unable to answer the riddles
the ogre set, was turned into a pillar of stone.

The younger brother, finding the knife rusted and dull, set off in search of his brother, but the same thing happened.

Finally the only son of the widow's neighbor, a kindly, generous lad, set off seeking the other two. He also encountered Red Etin, but was aided by a fairy woman who told him the answers to the riddles, and was able to behead the ogre and change the stone pillars back into men.

The ogre had captured and held prisoner a number of beautiful women, including a Scottish princess:

"The Red-Etin of Ireland
Once lived in Bellygan,
And stole King Malcolm's daughter,
The King of fair Scotland..."

As in all the best tales, as a reward for her rescue and for freeing the land of the monster, the King gave the young man his daughter's hand in marriage.

Mermaids

~

The mermaids of Scotland are a little different from maidens with fish tails instead of legs who lure sailors to their doom, as they are usually portrayed.

They are still noted for their lovely singing, but Scottish mermaids are human in form (although their skins are covered with silvery scales). And far from trying to harm humans, they are generally favorably disposed to them, sometimes even giving medical advice to their human neighbors.

The mermaid who lived near Port Glasgow advised the people to use a decoction of nettles and mugwort as a remedy for the consumption that was slowly killing off the young women in the neighborhood (unfortunately there is no readily available record as to whether they took her advice, or, if so, whether it was successful . . .) Nevertheless, nettles boiled in water make an effective antiseptic and anesthetic drink, and mugwort tea is traditionally used as a treatment for rheumatism and fevers as well as gynecological problems, so the mermaid obviously had some knowledge of herbal medicine!

Her sister mermaid who haunted a pool near Dalbeattie also used to offer advice to the appreciative residents, until a Bible-wielding Christian woman living nearby overturned the rock on which the mermaid always sat.

The woman's only child was found dead the next morning, and in retribution the pool was poisoned with filth until the mermaid was forced to leave, cursing with barrenness, as she did so, the family that had so ill-treated her.

Whether the rest of the community learned tolerance from the affair isn't known, but a similar incident took place at Knockdolian Castle, where the lady of the house ordered the mermaid's rock destroyed because her music kept the baby awake. The family is now extinct . . .

The Mermaid

To yon false stream that, near the sea,
Hides many an elf and bottomless pool,
One bright fine day, to wash and rest,
There came a knight that was a fool.

When, as he washed, sounds came so sweet
From every rock and tree;
His fate was cast, twas him it doomed
The mermaid's face to see.

From 'neath a rock, soon, soon she rose,
And stately on she swam,
Stopped in the midst, and beckoned, and
    sang,
To him to stretch his hand.

Golden shone the yellow links
That round her neck she'd twine;
Her eyes did best the sky's bright blue,
Her lips did mock red wine;

The smile upon her bonnie cheek
Was sweeter than the bee;
Her voice excelled the birdie's song
Upon the birchen tree.

The mermaid clasped his outstretched hand
And into the depths she dove –
About the stream his wraith's now seen,
Bemoaning her false love . . .

The Kindly Brownie

The Laird of Culzean once met a tiny lad, who begged a mug of ale for his sick mother. The kindly laird commanded his butler to give the lad all he needed – but after the first barrel-full of ale had disappeared into the tiny mug the servant thought it best to consult his master. Being told to carry on, he opened another barrel, but after a few spoonfuls the mug was full, and the lad, thanking the laird, went his way.

Years later the laird was captured in Flanders during the war, and languished in a dungeon. On the eve of his execution the prison door opened of its own accord and the lad, no older than when they'd first met, bade the laird leave the dungeon. Once outside he swept the laird onto his shoulder and in the blink of an eye set him down before his own castle gate. The laird was speechless, but the lad smiled and, just before vanishing, said –

"One good turn deserves another –
That's for being kind to my mother."

Industrious Giants

Near Kingussie, south over the mountains from Loch Ness, is the Great Cave of Lynchat.

Tradition has it that the cave was dug in a single night by a race of giants, the males wielding the shovels and pickaxes while the giantesses carried the debris down to the river. When the cave was finished, they lived there for a while, dealing peaceably with the few humans who came their way – and archaeological research has concluded that the cave was indeed a dwelling place in the past, though probably not that of giants!

A descendant of these giants is said to still live in Glenmore Forest, not far from Lynchat. Once the terror of travelers, he now protects the wildlife there, blessing those who deal gently with Mother Nature – and cursing those who don't . . .

The Loch Ness Monster

~

Loch Ness is an awesome place, long, deep and narrow: the steep mountains of Glen Mor on either side can act as a funnel for the wind, whipping the surface of the loch into furious storms. With its air of brooding mystery, it is not surprising to find that it is the home of a supernatural being . . .

Nessie, as the monster is affectionately known, is an ancient phenomenon. The first recorded sighting dates from around 565 AD, when one of St Columba's monks came face to face with the creature while swimming in the loch.

The saint commanded the monster let him be, since when, although its appearance has frightened not a few visitors to the area, the monster has never caused a human any harm.

There have been numerous reported sightings of the monster throughout the centuries, but until recent times these have relied more on word of mouth than any more concrete evidence. Then in 1933 the first photograph of an apparent "monster" was taken by Hugh Gray, a local man out for a Sunday walk . . .

More sightings followed, and later other, clearer photographs. Monster-hunters flocked to the area, and the Loch Ness Investigation Bureau was set up to research the phenomenon. Sonar traces of something very large and solid were recorded around the beginning of the 1970s, and more photographs and eyewitness accounts were added to the growing body of evidence.

Descriptions of the monster are surprisingly consistent: between 40 and 70 feet long, dark gray, with large flippers, a long tail, and a small, squarish head on a long neck. It sounds, in fact, very much like a plesiosaurus, a water-dwelling reptile that died out (as far as we know) 70 million years ago – rather like the coelacanth, which was also believed to be long-extinct until one was caught in 1938 ...

Of course, there were many attempts to explain "Nessie" away – that it was a giant otter, a giant eel, a deer swimming across the loch, even an elephant swimming under water (its raised trunk being mistaken for the neck and head). Several hoaxes – including the decomposing body of a dead elephant seal, a man-made construction of plastic sacks, sticks and string, and the discovery that some of the "scientific" evidence was also spurious – have added to the skepticism with which stories of the monster are viewed by the scientific community.

Nevertheless, the many local eyewitness reports are undeniable. Despite all attempts to explain away the creature, it seems that there really IS something strange under the dark waters ...

The Roane

Close cousins to the selkies, whom they resemble, the roane live much further out in the seas around the Scottish coast, and are very rarely seen.

Their seal-skins are pure white, or sometimes golden, and they choose the wildest and most inaccessible beaches and islands on which to come ashore. Both male and female roane delight in dance, and a company dancing on a beach of pale sand under a full moon is a sight any artist would give much to see.

Unfortunately, the roane are intensely protective of their privacy and always post guards at such gatherings. At the slightest hint of a human presence, the alarm is given and the entire group slip swiftly into their pelts and away, and may never be seen at that spot again.

A Mischievous Sprite

~

The Shellycoat, a small water spirit whose presence was announced by the clattering of the coat of shells he wore, was known for his exasperating but essentially harmless pranks.

Shellycoat was kin to the Brownies rather than the fairies and haunted many rocks around the Scottish coast. A favorite haunt was a large rock at Leith, where children used to gather to taunt the creature – presumably in the hope that he would appear to them. Not that anyone ever did see him: while not necessarily invisible, Shellycoat was always heard, not seen.

The creature had a fondness, like the will o' the wisp, for leading travelers astray. A favorite trick was to pretend to be drowning: the Shellycoat would move further and further upriver, making the would-be rescuers follow him for hours, until he reached some wild, desolate place. There he gave up the pretence and left the humans stranded miles from anywhere: the last they heard was a loud, bubbling laughter fading away into the distance.

One tradition has it that, when tired after performing some particularly strenuous piece of mischief, Shellycoat would take off his coat and hide it safely under a rock while he rested. Like the selkies, this would render him powerless, and anyone finding and keeping his coat could command his obedience.

The only problem was that, given the sprite's mischievous nature, any task he was forced to perform would rebound on the human who demanded it!

Island Trolls

~

Where the Fey-Folk of the Scottish mainland were usually beautiful, the trolls (or trows) that came to the Shetland islands with the Norse settlers were misshapen and ugly!

They were also very rich. Trolls, like their close cousins the dwarfs, had easy access to the wealth that lies in the ground, both as gold and precious gems. Also like dwarfs, trolls were exclusively male – no female trolls were ever born. They were forced, therefore, to steal away human girls or women for their wives.

Despite their riches, they were so ugly that no woman would willingly partner a troll. And, because the children of such unions were always male and always ugly, the trolls would try to exchange them for human children, taking pretty babies from their cradles and leaving in their place ugly, whining changelings, or sometimes just a carved log in the shape of a child.

Fortunately, though, trolls were only really dangerous at night: they turned to stone if caught in daylight, and sometimes even shattered if touched by bright sunlight. The creatures could also be appeased by gifts of food or drink left at the entrances to their caves or mounds – they were particularly fond of mead, the honey-based liquor brewed since ancient times – and wise islanders could learn spells to keep themselves and their homes safe at night.

Like many of the Fey-Folk, trolls were fond of music, and it was possible, if one were brave and talented enough, to charm a troll into parting with his treasure in return for a song – but this was a perilous business and not for the faint-hearted. Failure to please could be, literally, fatal!

The Elfin Knight – and the Maiden
who was his Match!
~

The Elfin Knight stands on yon hill
(Blow, blow, blow winds, blow!)
Blowin' his horn baith loud and shrill
(And the wind has blown my plaid away!)

"I wish he'd kiss me, not that horn,
And hold me in his hands sae warm."

"To prove ye're not tae young," he said
"Ye'll do some chores ere we'll be wed!

"Ye must make for me a linen shirt
Wi' no' a stitch o' needlework,

"And ye must wash it in a well
Where water neither sprang nor fell,

"And ye must dry it on a hawthorn
That hasnae bloomed since Adam was born."

And she: "If that courtesy I do for ye
There's one that ye must do for me.

"I have an acre of meadow lawn
That ye must plough wi' just your horn.

"Without seed it must be sown
And wheat reaped wi' a sheep's shank bone.

"Bind it wi' Robin Redbreast's feather
And thresh it in a shoe wi' no leather.

"And if ye do well all this work
Come back to me and I'll make your shirt!"

"Since ye've measured these riddles fine,"
Said he, "Ne'er doubt – ye shall be mine!"

The Borders Bogeyman

~

Hermitage Castle, on the Borders, was once the home of the evil Lord Soulis, whose cruelty was legendary even for the four-teenth century . . .

Soulis was a treacherous man, conspiring against the king, persecuting the neighboring lords, and mistreating his vassals mercilessly. There was a tradition in the area that he had bored holes in the shoulders of his serfs the more easily to harness them to the carts full of the stones used to build his castle (it is also said that the demons with whom Soulis had regular meetings helped with the construction).

Lord Soulis had a familiar, a grotesque old man in shape with fiery red eyes and sharp talons. The familiar was known as Redcap or Bloodycap for his habit of butchering travelers and catching their blood in his hat. Legend has it that while Redcap remained bound to Soulis, the Lord would never be killed by the sword or by hanging.

Confident that his life was charmed, Lord Soulis continued with his villainies, until the king, weary of the endless complaints of the neighboring barons, exclaimed:

"Boil him if you please, but let me hear no more of him!"

Eager to take advantage of the king's irritation, the barons hurried to do as he suggested before he could change his mind. On their return home they seized Lord Soulis, transported him to the ancient stone circle of Ninestane Ring – and boiled him to death rolled up in a sheet of lead!

The familiar's protection did not apply to this ordeal, and Redcap was forced to allow Soulis to perish. But there are those who say he still haunts the castle, awaiting another master.

The Great Scottish Wizard

~

"That other there, who looks so lean
   and small
In the flanks, was Michael Scot, who
   verily
Knew every trick of the art magical."
                          (canto XX, 115–7)

So spoke Virgil in Dante's "Inferno," the first
part of *The Divine Comedy* – Scot was
numbered amongst the sorcerers in the
Eighth Circle of Hell!

Scot's reputation was considerable. He was
said to have the power of magical flight, once
traveling to Rome so swiftly that he arrived at
the Pope's palace with Highland snow still on
his cloak.

It is believed that Scot built what is now
known as Hadrian's Wall, with the Devil's
help. According to the legend, he had devils

attending on him during the construction. One devil in particular was especially persistent, pestering his master for increasingly difficult tasks. The wizard responded first by having him split Eildon Hill into three separate peaks, and when that wasn't enough, by setting him to twisting ropes from sand at the mouth of the river Tweed (where, according to tradition, the devil is still laboring . . .)

Michael Scot was born sometime around the end of the twelfth century, and records show that he was a cleric and a scholar, renowned for his proficiency in Latin, Hebrew and Arabic. He worked as a translator for a while at the beginning of the thirteenth century. He was also a skilled astrologer – a science he equated with magic, although in his own writings he condemned magical practice – and a philosopher and physician. For some time he lived at the court of the Holy Roman Emperor Frederick II.

Perhaps not a wizard, but certainly a highly respected man in his time.

Scot is said to be buried in Melrose Abbey – a surprising place for one reputed to have trafficked with the Devil!

The Salmon-woman of the Highlands

~

The little-known ceasg is a unique type of mermaid, whose upper body is that of a mature and lovely woman but whose lower body is shaped like a salmon's tail.

Her voice is enchantingly musical and soothing. At home in both salt and fresh water, she is famed, like the salmon, for her gift of wisdom, and if in a good humor may grant three wishes to any human lucky enough to encounter her.

Simply glimpsing the ceasg can bring good fortune. If one is lucky enough to actually meet her, however, it is vitally important that any wishes be wise and sensible ones, as the ceasg has no patience with stupidity or selfishness, and will happily lure the foolish wisher into deep water to drown . . .

Thomas the Rhymer

Thomas was making music with his lute on the lower slopes of the southernmost of the Eildon hills, when out from the trees rode a lady of ethereal beauty, dressed in green silk and mounted upon a snow-white mare . . .

Struck by her radiance, the young poet hastened to meet her, thinking that maybe he had been blessed with a vision of the Queen of Heaven. But she was the Queen of Faerie, and emboldened by this knowledge, Thomas begged a kiss. At first she resisted, warning the poet that a kiss would bind him to her for seven years – but Thomas desired her, and played sweet music to charm her, and finally she dismounted and allowed him his way . . .

Commanding Thomas to follow her, she led him to the Otherworld, where he lived in luxury and delight for what seemed to be just seven days, but was in the real world seven years. In that time he was obedient to his Queen, speaking to no one but her, and joining her subjects in their revels. At the end of the time he returned to his townsfolk, who had long ago given him up for lost.

At his leaving, the Queen had blessed (though some would say cursed) him with the inability to tell a lie, and in his remaining earthly life he became renowned as a prophet.

In his seventy-eighth year, at his annual feast for his kinsfolk, a pair of milk-white deer came to fetch him back to the Otherworld – where, if the tales of other visitors are to be believed, he lives to this day, still charming the fair-folk with his songs . . .

Thomas the Rhymer

~

True Thomas lay on yon grassy bank
When he beheld a lady fine,
And at her horse's silky mane
Hung fifty silver bells and nine.

True Thomas he took off his hat
And bowed him low upon his knee:
"All hail, thou mighty Queen of Heaven!
For your peer on earth I never did see."

"Oh no, oh, no, Thomas, not Heaven
But the Queen of Faerie,
Drawn by thy sweet music, Thomas –
Now ye must go with me . . ."

She turned about her milk-white steed,
And took true Thomas up behind,
And whenever her bridle chimed and rang,
The steed flew swifter than the wind . . .

At length into Elfland they came,
And there was revel, game and play,
Lovely ladies, fair and free,
Dancing with all in rich array . . .

"Dress thee Thomas, for thou must go –
Here no longer may you be,
Tomorrow a fiend from hell itself
Amongst these folk shall choose his fee –
Thou art a fair and noble man,
I know full well he will choose thee . . ."

She brought him again to the Eildon tree,
And Thomas a sorry man was he,
"Must we part for ever?
My lady, tell it me . . ."

"Nay, my Thomas, we shall yet meet
When thou art old and hoar,
And thou shall return to Faerie-land
To leave there nevermore . . ."

Scotland's Stonehenge

The megaliths at Callanish on the Isle of Lewis may lack the lintels of the famous trilithons at Stonehenge, but they are contemporary with their celebrated cousins, and are quite as mysterious.

One popular legend explains the fifty-odd gray standing stones as being the effigies of giants (some are 12 feet tall) who were turned to stone for making merry in defiance of St Kiaran's call to Christianity. The shape of the petrified arrangement – a traditional Christian cross with a central circle, making a Celtic Cross – was a clear warning of the power of the new religion.

A more picturesque local version tells of a sacred king bringing the stones from across the sea. He was always accompanied by a flock of wrens, and wore a magical cloak of bright-hued and iridescent feathers. The stones themselves were erected at his command by a crew of men as black as the night sky.

The monument, overlooking Loch Roag, is on what is now a windswept moorland ridge, but when it was built, some 4,000 years ago, the landscape was far less bleak and the climate much warmer.

The circle of thirteen stones has a central monolith, which is the tallest of all and still the focus for Beltaine rites. It is rumored cryptically that Callanish was used by Celtic Druids more recently than any other site.

The long "arm" of the cross is a ceremonial avenue 270 feet long, which approaches the circle from the north-northeast and would have brought the ancients to a remarkable vista – that of the full moon at midsummer barely rising two degrees above the horizon before sinking again behind the tallest peak on the island.

Rarer Brownies

In the wilder reaches of the Highlands and the once-great forests of Scotland live little-known creatures, half-fairy and half-goat, somewhat like the satyrs of the Mediterranean countries but much less tame. These are the Uruisg, the spirits of the forest.

The Uruisg are wild, shy, and can be savage if cornered, but if you manage to make friends with them, they can be extremely helpful. They will protect the household and perform many outdoor tasks for the family, asking only the occasional meal and a kind word as reward. A word of warning, however, they are very easily offended.

Once common on the islands around the Scottish coast, and sometimes seen in the far north of the mainland, was the Gruagach, a Brownie woman whose particular task was to guard livestock at night. She had to be given a mug of milk as payment, however, or she would help herself to the finest cows – and her appetite was prodigious!

A Scottish Yeti . . . ?

~

The flat, bare summit of Ben Macdhui (the blue mountain) is well known to walkers in the Cairngorms. Maybe a little less well known is the mysterious figure that haunts the snowy slopes . . .

A monstrous figure half-hidden by mist, or glimpsed on the horizon as a dark shadow against the sunlit snow or the sky, is the lumbering presence known as the Big Gray Man of Ben Macdhui.

Although there are no detailed descriptions of the apparition, the Big Gray Man has been seen by numerous climbers. Others have seen his footprints, or, on a clear and windless day, heard a distant sound of ponderous heavy feet crunching through the snow.

The Body Snatchers

~

Life may have been cheap in the nineteenth century, but death wasn't!

At that time, each medical school was only allowed the body of one executed criminal per year for dissection in anatomy class. Of course, one body wasn't nearly enough, and a thriving new trade sprang up – that of "resurrectionist" (a polite name for graverobbers!) Anatomists offered £14 per corpse – quite a fortune in those days.

Despite the dangers of being caught, numerous people, many of them anatomy students themselves, gave in to temptation. William Burke and William Hare, Irish laborers living in Edinburgh, however, hit on a less strenuous method of earning the money . . .

Rather than dig up recently interred bodies, they set about providing their own, luring victims into Hare's boarding house, plying them with whisky, then smothering them to death!

Between February and October of 1828 they provided Edinburgh University's medical school with somewhere between thirteen and thirty fresh corpses. They had a narrow escape when a student recognized the girl he was dissecting, but it wasn't until a lodger became curious about the sudden disappearance of a fellow resident, and actually found the body, that the pair were finally captured.

Hare saved his own life by giving evidence against his erstwhile colleague, and later left Scotland. Burke, however, was found guilty orf murder and hanged on 29 January 1829. In an ironic twist of fate, his body was delivered to the medical school to be dissected in anatomy class.

The Fachan of Glen Etive

~

At the head of Loch Etive in the southwest of the Highlands is Glen Etive, a long narrow valley bordered in part by steep mountains, and the haunt of one of the strangest figures in Scottish folklore ...

Little is known about the Fachan, apart from its unique appearance: the monster has only one eye, one arm, and one leg. It is rumored that it assumed this guise either in envy of the Druids or to mock them – Druids were said to stand on one leg with one eye closed and one arm outstretched when performing their rituals.

Whatever the reason, it is unwise to be caught after nightfall in the Glen, especially at Hallowe'en – unless you want to risk catching sight of the monster, of course!

Some Good Advice

The Fey-Folk are very powerful, but there are some objects and elements that can protect ordinary mortals from their influence.

Foremost is iron, in any shape or form. The Good People cannot abide the metal – in some cases it can prove fatal to them, but even if it is not, they will refuse to stay in a place, or near a person, bearing iron.

Malevolent fairies are usually unable to cross running water – a tradition later extended to vampires. The obvious exceptions are the kelpies and the sea-folk.

Rowan is a sure defense against magical powers, whether good or ill. Rowan twigs or branches hung in dwellings or over entrances will prevent the Folk from using their abilities – but will not actually harm them, and so is a useful, friendly way to ward off mischief!

The Magical Garden . . .

~

On the Moray Firth, further north than Moscow and far from the nurturing warmth of the Gulf Stream, is the extraordinary community of Findhorn.

Started in 1963 as a small garden on the windswept, sandy peninsula near Forres, the first family to live there gradually grew into a self-sustaining, richly flourishing community living in perfect accord with the natural world. It should have been impossible, given the infertility of the soil and the frequent 70 mph winds that struck the unprotected headland – yet somehow everything planted there thrived.

The reason was cooperation, in its truest and deepest form. The "devas" (sentient life-forces) of the plants were "speaking" to their human colleagues, guiding them, advising them literally how best to make their garden grow – and not just the physical garden around them. The individual members of the community were taught how to develop and evolve within themselves, gaining extraordinary insight and abilities along the way (one method of encouraging the plants to flourish from the poor soil, in the earliest days, was to channel mental energy into them, literally "willing" them to grow).

The Findhorn community has an enviable awareness of the interconnected-ness of all life on the planet, and a deep concern for the environmental health of the world. And whether you believe in devas or not, the Findhorn practices work at Findhorn – as they would work anywhere – for anyone prepared to open themselves to the mysterious forces at work in nature.

ANIMAL LORE

~

Whether we eat them, hunt them, watch them or keep them as pets, animals are an everyday part of our lives. Sometimes they bring good luck, sometimes bad; sometimes they can even prophesy the future. The following pages give some instances of the folklore surrounding the animal kingdom in Scotland.

Winged Souls

~

Butterflies, those beautiful harbingers of summer, should never be harmed – they may be the souls of the recently dead . . .

In ancient times there was no belief in heaven or hell. The souls of the dead returned to the Summerlands (sometimes called Tir Nan Og – the Land of the Young) to rest for a while before being reborn as human infants. The Summerlands was exactly as its name suggests, a bright blessed place, where life continued much as on earth, but happier and not cursed with disease, distress or death (similar to the Otherworld of the Fey-Folk: in fact, the two are often confused in folklore).

To make the transition from earthly life to Summerlands homecoming, souls some-times assumed the form of butterflies – creatures that would be perfectly at home in the place of everlasting summer. To hurt or kill one, therefore, may be to cause great distress to the person it had been. Even worse, it could bring down grievous misfortune on the head of the person doing the harm . . .

Butterflies could also, on rare occasions, bring great joy. A golden butterfly hovering near a dying man could restore him to health and guarantee good fortune for the future.

Such butterflies, alas, are very, very rare!

Ladybird

Ladybird, Ladybird, here on my hand,
Ladybird, Ladybird, wi' red cloak sae grand,
Rise up and fly over firth and fell,
Fly over loch and brook-laced dell,
Fly over moor and flowery mead,
Fly over living and fly over dead,
Fly over corn and fly over lea,
Fly over river and fly over sea,
Fly tae the east or fly tae the west,
But show where he is who'll love me the best!

The Seven Whistlers

~

Woe to the man who ignores the haunting cry of the curlew . . . !

The piteous whistling call of these birds foretells death and disaster, and it's a wise man who bides at home the day they appear. The omens are especially bad if their cries are heard at night.

They are particularly fateful for sailors and fishermen, who hear in their calls the voices of drowned comrades, crying out from their watery graves to warn of an approaching storm or other peril. Many a shipwreck or drowning followed when the Seven Whistlers' alarms were disregarded.

It is said in some places that there are in fact only six Whistlers, who are searching for the seventh – and should they ever find their missing colleague, the world will come to an end . . .

The Herald of Spring

~

The Eurasian cuckoo, unlike its American cousin, is probably best known for its habit of laying its eggs in the nests of other birds and ejecting the other inhabitants within hours of hatching. This has led to it being viewed with suspicion as a deceitful and unscrupulous bird. However, its intimate association with brighter weather and burgeoning vegetation (in ancient times the cuckoo was thought to actually bring the spring with it when it reappeared after its migration to warmer climes over winter) also makes it a bird of good omen.

In the Highlands, cuckoos were associated with the Fey-Folk. They were believed to spend the winter safely hidden away in fairy hills where they joined in the fairy revels, adding their voices to the dance. The fact that the fairy Otherworld was a place of beauty and enchantment would explain the briefness of the cuckoo's stay in Scotland – five months at most. It is little wonder that the bird would only reluctantly leave its fabulous winter home and then hurry back again once its job of heralding the spring was done!

It is very lucky to be out walking, especially in the hills, when the first call of the cuckoo is heard – as long as you have money in your pocket! Any coins you have should be turned over to allow them to increase in the coming year. It is important, also, to count the number of times the cuckoo calls. This number used to represent the years of life left to the hearer, but these days they are more likely to be counted to see how many months of the year will be blessed with good fortune.

Winged Things...

~

If a cock crows after darkness falls
Catch the bird and hold your breath
If its feet feel warm expect good news
If cold then ye must await a death.

A dove that circles thrice over head
Will bear ye tae heaven when ye are dead.

The Wren –

Misfortunes! Misfortunes! Aye, mair than
    ten
Smite any who vex the Queen o' Heaven's
    hen!

Wrens fight fully as keenly as cranes!

Game for a Lark?

Anyone tempted to harry or harm one of these beautiful songsters should heed an ancient warning...

Under the tongues of these sweetly tuneful little birds are three dark spots, and these blots will grow on the tongue of anyone who causes them injury or distress. Not only that, but each dark spot will bring with it a dire curse that will blight the life of the evil-minded wretch!

The Devil's Bird

~

"One's sorrow,
Twa's mirth,
Three's a weddin',
Four's a birth,
Five's a christenin'
Six a death,
Seven's heaven,
Eight is hell,
And nine's the very Devil himsel'."

So chant even otherwise perfectly unsuperstitious people at the sight of a tiding of magpies!

The magpie has been seen as an ominous bird since earliest times, and is believed, especially in the north of Scotland, to carry a drop of the Devil's blood under its tongue: it is thus very dangerous to harm one of these creatures, since it may pass on this blood to the one injuring it and thence bring down a curse upon the ill-doer's head. And woe betide anyone who actually kills a magpie . . .

In some areas magpies were also thought to be witches' familiars, and it was vital not to speak while they were nearby in case they carried secrets back to their masters which could be used in malicious spells.

A single magpie, flying over a person's head or chattering persistently around a house, foretells death, and to encounter a single magpie in one's day-to-day life is unlucky. The bad luck may be averted, however, by bowing to the bird, spitting after it, or crossing one's fingers (or oneself). Equally, seeing two birds together is an omen of good luck – but only if they are saluted in a similar way, otherwise the good fortune will not arrive.

The Swan of Death

~

For centuries the Kirkpatrick family of Dumfries were haunted by a swan which appeared as a herald of approaching death . . .

The legend had a much happier beginning. The fourteenth-century tower-house of Closeburn Castle, the ancestral home of the Kirkpatricks, was also the summer home of a pair of swans who frequented the loch surrounding the castle. On two occasions their arrival coincided with the sudden and unexpected recovery from serious illness of members of the Kirkpatrick family, and the graceful birds quickly became regarded as the bringers of good luck.

A pair of swans returned to grace the loch every summer for the next one hundred and fifty years, bringing, it was believed, good fortune and prosperity with them. Then Robert Kirkpatrick, the heir, a young and cynical lad not yet thirteen, saw Shakespeare's *The Merchant of Venice* in Edinburgh . . .

Struck particularly by the play's reference to the swan-song:

> . . . he makes a swan-like end,
> Fading in music . . .
> *Act III, Scene II, 44–5*

he killed one of the swans with his crossbow to see if the legend of its final lovely song was true. Of course, it was not. Terrified of the possible consequences of his act, he buried the bird in the castle grounds and mentioned it to no one. When the birds did not return the following year, the family assumed, sadly, that they had died while abroad. A little later in the summer, however, a single swan appeared on the loch, with a blood-red mark on its breast, and within a week the head of the family sickened and died.

From that time forth, tradition has it, the swan was always seen just before the death of a member of the family.

The Faithful Little Dog

~

On a modest pedestal on the corner of George IV Bridge and Candlemaker Row, in Edinburgh's Old Town, stands the statue of a small dog, the city's tribute to the love and faithfulness of "man's best friend" . . .

This is Bobby, a Skye terrier (an ancient Scottish breed originally used to hunt foxes and badgers), who, after his master John Gray's death in 1858, for fourteen years watched over the grave in the adjacent Greyfriars Churchyard. The little dog became a familiar sight and was viewed with much affection by the regular passers-by who kept him fed and watered. He died on the grave and was buried nearby. The commemorative stone at the cemetery entrance reads:

"Let his loyalty and devotion
be a lesson to us all."

The Lucky Horseshoe

～

Nailing an iron horseshoe upon the outside of the door of a barn, stable or house, prevents evil spirits and witchery from entering.

Even better, by fixing it with three nails, heel uppermost (e.g. in the shape of the letter U), the shoe will become a vessel to keep good luck from draining away.

If you are lucky enough to find a horseshoe in your path, pick it up, spit on it and toss it over your left shoulder, all the while strongly imagining a wish coming true, and it shall surely come to pass.

But remember –

If wishes were horses, beggars would ride!

To a Mouse

Wee, sleeket, cowran, tim'rous beastie,
O' what a panic's in thy breastie!
Thou need na start awa sae hasty
    Wi' bickering brattle!
I wad be loath to run an' chase thee
    Wi' murdering pattle!

I'm truly sorry man's dominion
Has broken Nature's social union,
An' justifies that ill opinion
    Which makes thee startle
At me, thy poor, earth-born companion
    An' fellow mortal!

Thou saw the fields laid bare an' waste,
An' weary winter comin' fast,
An' cozy here, beneath the blast,
    Thou thought to dwell,
Til, crash! the cruel plough-share passed
    Out through thy cell.

But Mousie, thou art not alone
In proving foresight may be vain:
The best-laid schemes o' Mice an' Men
    Gang oft agley,
And leave us nought but grief an' pain,
    For promis'd joy!

Still thou art blessed, compared wi' me!
The present only touches thee:
But och! I backwards cast my eye,
    On prospects drear!
An' forward, though I canna see,
    I guess an' fear . . .

Robert Burns

The Spider and Robert the Bruce

~

Robert known as the Bruce became king at one of Scotland's numerous turbulent points in history, when conflict with the English was at a peak. After one particularly bloody battle and defeat at the hands of the English, Robert was forced to take shelter in a damp, gloomy cave to escape the pursuing army.

His own army broken, his sovereignty at stake, and seeing no way out, close to despair he sat and pondered his fate. Unable even to light a fire for fear the English would discover his hiding place, he finally found himself distracted by a tiny spider, weaving a web in a chink in the cave wall. The wind blowing through the narrow space kept tearing the fragile web, but the spider resolutely carried on trying, until finally it completed its task.

Heartened by the symbolism, and with (or

so they say!) those famous words, "If at first ye dinnae succeed, try, try agin!", Robert went forth again, determined to succeed. On 24 June 1314, at the Battle of Bannock-burn, his tiny army defeated that of Edward II, a battle which eventually led to Scotland's independence – and the spider passed into legend.

It's a victory still remembered today in what has become Scotland's unofficial National Anthem, "The Flower of Scotland."

O flower of Scotland,
When will we see your like again,
That fought and died for
Your wee bit hill and glen,
And stood against him,
Proud Edward's army,
And sent him homewards
To think again.

Holy Cow

~

It is a notable sign of good fortune, which will last a full twelve months, if the very first calf of the "muckle coo" (a traditional Highland cow with long horns and a long coat of shaggy red hair) that you see in the spring of the year is facing toward you.

The same, incidentally, is also said of lambs and foals!

~

They call a calf a hefty beast
That never met a cow!

~

He never lost a cow, that wept for a pin.

Animal Proverbs

~

Nae dog howls if ye beat it wi' a bone.

~

Lightning ne'er strikes where swallows nest.

~

If ye wish tae live and thrive
Let the spider run alive.

~

The mother o' mischief is nae bigger
Than a midge's wing . . .

A Merry Dance

Cats have been regarded with suspicion and awe from time immemorial: sometimes as a beast of evil omen and the familiar of witches, and sometimes as man's helper, like the farm cat in the following nursery rhyme:

> A cat stood singing outside the barn
> Wi' a blaring bagpipe under its arm,
> It frightened away a wee brown mouse
> And a humble bee moved intae her house!

Of course, anyone would prefer the honey-making bee to the destructive brown mouse – probably even Robert Burns!

FEASTS AND FESTIVALS

Traditionally, like most people the Scots observed the eight major festivals of the natural year: Imbolg (1 February); the vernal (spring) equinox; Beltaine (May Day); the Midsummer solstice; Lughnassadh, pronounced "LOO-na-sad" (Lammas, 1 August); the autumn (fall) equinox; Samhain, pronounced "SAH-wen" (Hallowe'en); and Yule (the winter solstice).

Of course, some of these were seen as more important than others – and some of them were later Christianized. Nevertheless, many customs remain from ancient times. And the Scots also have several festivals unique to themselves!

Bringing in the New Year

~

The clattering of pots and pans, the ringing of church bells, the cheery noise of drunken revelry – it could easily be argued that the festival of Hogmanay is more important to the Scots than any other in the diary! It celebrates the end of the Old Calendrical Year and the beginning of the New.

Certain practices must be followed, though, to ensure good luck. The house must be thoroughly cleaned before midnight: it is unlucky to do any kind of domestic work, or take rubbish out of the house, on New Year's Day. Nor must any washing of clothes take place on 1 January, for fear of "washin' one o' the family awa'."

In the Highlands the hearthfire lit on Old Year's Night must stay alight until 2 January, or bad luck will follow: in other places, a candle is lit at sunset on 31 December and kept burning until sunrise on New Year's Day (other candles are lit from the first as it burns down).

Another custom is that of throwing a silver coin through the open door in the first three minutes of the New Year: the coin must remain where it falls throughout the year to ensure that the household will never be short of money. These days, this usually means pulling up the carpet and hiding the coin underneath it!

The most important custom, though, is "First Footing" – the first person through the door after midnight must be someone dark-haired (dark-complexioned is allowable) and carrying a lump of coal, a piece of shortbread and a small bottle of whisky, to symbolize that the household will have warmth, food and good times all through the coming year.

Auld Lang Syne

"Auld lang syne" means "times long since" or "the good old days" . . . The song is always sung at Hogmanay.

> Should auld acquaintance be forgot,
> And never brought to mind?
> Should auld acquaintance be forgot,
> And auld lang syne?

> (Chorus)
> For auld lang syne, my dear,
> For auld lang syne,
> We'll take a cup o' kindness yet,
> For auld lang syne!

> And surely ye'll raise your pint-mug,
> And surely I'll raise mine,
> And we'll take a cup o' kindness yet
> For auld lang syne!

> (Chorus)

We two hae run about the braes,
And pulled the daisies fine,
But we've wandered many a weary mile
Since auld lang syne.

(Chorus)

We two hae paddled in the burn
From morning sun til dine,
But seas between us broad have roared
Since auld lang syne.

(Chorus)

And there's a hand my trusty friend,
And gie's a hand o' thine,
And we'll take a right good friendly sup
For auld lang syne!

(Chorus)

Robert Burns

Burns Night

~

Burns Night (25 January) celebrates the man who is considered Scotland's most popular, if not greatest, poet, Robert Burns (1759–96). Credited with the creation of the traditional New Year's Eve song, "Auld Lang Syne," Burns was as successful as a poet as he was unsuccessful as a farmer.

Burns Night is celebrated in grand style, with the haggis piped to the table by a piper dressed in traditional tartan kilt and sporran, and accompanied by plentiful supplies of "tatties" (potatoes), "neeps" (the orange root vegetable variously called swede or turnip pureed with butter and freshly ground black pepper) and "nips" (shots of good whisky).

The haggis is toasted and "addressed," and the meal punctuated by speeches and recitations. The festivities carry on as long as there is whisky left to drink, and the evening usually finishes with a resounding chorus or two of "Auld Lang Syne."

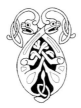

Address to a Haggis

~

Fair fa' your honest, sonsie face,
Great chieftain o' the puddin-race!
Aboon them a' ye tak your place,
    Painch, tripe, or thairm:
Weel are ye wordy of a grace
    As lang's my arm.

The groaning trencher there ye fill,
Your hurdies like a distant hill,
Your pin wad help to mend a mill
    In time o' need,
While thro' your pores the dew distil
    Like amber bead.

Robert Burns

Hunting the Wild Haggis

~

A vitally important date in the Scottish Country Calendar is 31 June, the one day in the year when hunting of wild haggis is legal...

The wild haggis is generally a shy and solitary nocturnal creature, much given to skulking in the inaccessible reaches of the Grampian Mountains. There have, though, been instances of rogues who attack remote villages, but the locals play the bagpipes to scare them away. During the rutting season, however, vast hordes of the beasts assemble in the glens and on the lochsides.

Their cries (a high-pitched squeal rather like the eerie wailing of distant bagpipes) can be heard for miles, echoing up and down the glens and striking fear into the hearts of lonely crofters...

The hunt starts at midnight on 30 June.

Huntsmen clad in kilt and sporran gather to toast each other's luck in whisky before letting loose the haggis-hounds – short-legged dogs specially bred to recognize the mating call of the wild haggis. The hunt ends strictly at midnight on 31 June.

The haggis – no more than thirteen per huntsman, to ensure they aren't completely wiped out – should be despatched with the traditional crossbow, and the spoils either cooked and eaten, or gutted and the skins made into bagpipes. However, particularly fine specimens may be made into sporrans, which are usually kept as heirlooms or sold for outrageous prices to unsuspecting tourists!

The Haggis Farmers of the Ochils

~

To the north of Stirling are the Ochil Hills, a wild place of rocks and heathery slopes.

Nestling amongst the hills are two adjoining haggis farms. Farmer MacDougal breeds his haggis with short right legs so that they can only graze clockwise around the hills, while his neighbor Farmer MacDonald favors the widdershins-grazing variety with the short left leg.

A carpenter in the village nearby makes award-winning haggis-stilts that are the pride of the region. They are used by haggis farmers both near and far to balance the length of their haggis-flocks' legs.

Since the haggis market is the main source of income for the area, Hamish the carpenter is, by ancient charter, allowed his pick of each year's stock of newborns.

Pipe in the Haggis!

This unique Scottish dish is perhaps the supreme example of the legendary Scottish thriftiness.

It is traditionally made from the heart, liver and lungs of a sheep or calf (in other words the parts that can't be used for much else). These ingredients are minced and mixed with onion, a handful or two of oatmeal, suet, spices, pepper, salt and meat stock. The resulting mixture is stuffed into the animal's own stomach and boiled for several hours until cooked. (Modern commercial varieties omit the stomach and are generally made from pork offal.)

The dish should be served with neeps and tatties (buttered swede or turnip and creamed potatoes).

To see or eat a haggis in a dream foretells prosperous times ahead – but if you cut and served it yourself, consider it a warning against the risks of behaving indiscreetly!

The Blue Hag of the Highlands

~

Imbolg (1 February) is usually the coldest time of year, and any celebrations that do take place center around the hearthfire. Imbolg is a good time for new beginnings.

In the Highlands, the frosts and storms of the Dark Year (1 November to 1 May) were believed to be caused by the Blue Hag, or Old Wife, a fearful elemental spirit.

Her hair is icy white, her face blue with the cold, and she strides the land wielding her gnarled staff, beating down the grass and freezing the ground. But at Imbolg, the Dark Year's halfway point, her power starts to wane, until May Day Eve, when she rests her staff under a holly tree, where no grass can grow, and she herself turns into a gray stone to await the next Hallowe'en . . .

There is a different legend, however, and one that is more appealing.

Instead of being a figure of terror, the Blue Hag is the Crone, the vessel of the wisdom of old age, who deals kindly with all those who seek her learning: in this guise she also protects deer (and wolves, when there were any left in Scotland). And, in an act heavily symbolic of the ancient belief in the cycle of birth—death—rebirth, she is able to change from the withered Crone of winter to the pure young beauty of spring, should a kind-hearted young man prove himself worthy . . .

May Day

~

The old name for May Day is Beltaine (sometimes spelled Beltane or Beal-teinne) – it means "Bel's Fire" and marks the beginning of the Light Year (summer and the flourishing growth and goodness that comes with the ascent of Bel, the Sun).

It is a magical time of the year, when the barriers between the ordinary world of mortals and the unseen world of Faerie grow very thin, but unlike Hallowe'en (Samhain, the beginning of the Dark Year), at Beltaine encounters with the Fey-Folk are most likely to be happy and tinged with good fortune. Nevertheless, many Scots, being canny folk, would hang hoops (later crosses) made of rowan twigs in the cow byres, just in case any mischievous member of the "Good People" should be tempted to steal the milk!

On Beltaine Eve all fires were extinguished and re-lit the following morning from the "needfire," which was kindled at sunrise on Beltaine itself. Out of doors, bonfires were lit, and entire herds of farm animals were driven between adjoining bonfires to ensure good health and a plentiful supply of milk or wool throughout the year. It was also considered good luck to leap the flames, and there is a tradition that women wishing to conceive should also – carefully! – jump over the bonfire.

These days, since the lighting of bonfires is problematic in many places, it has become customary in some areas simply to light a candle at sunrise – and for extra good fortune, to carry it three times deiseil or deosil (pronounced "JESH-ill": clockwise or following the direction of the sun) around the house. At the very least, rising early to watch the sunrise will bring good luck, especially from a high place. Arthur's Seat or Calton Hill in Edinburgh are renowned sites: in reality any east-facing high place will do!

Water also plays a significant role in the celebrations. Beltaine dew is particularly beneficial, and those wishing for success, health and happiness – and beauty! – should wash their faces in the sparkling water gathered at sunrise. (There are those that say if this comes from a thistle or a briar rose, so much the better . . .)

This is also an excellent time to pay a trip to one of the numerous healing wells or springs in Scotland. The Cloutie (or Saint Mary's) Well on Culloden Moor is perhaps the most famous, but there are many others: over one thousand, according to one authority, including Kinross Well, reputed to have cured Robert the Bruce's leprosy, Lady Well at Glamis, and Maiden's Well in the Ochil Hills. It is always wise to throw in a coin, preferably a silver one, as a tribute to the healing power of the water, and walking three times deiseil around the well increases its beneficial influence.

As a final note, it is traditional to cook a special bannock (small cake) of eggs, milk and oatmeal, to be eaten at breakfast to ensure there will always be food in the house in the coming year. Just make sure you leave a portion for the fairies!

Highland Games

Highland Games (more correctly Highland Gatherings!) take place between July and September up and down the length and breadth of Scotland – and in other parts of the world with a large population of Scots.

They are grand affairs, a commemoration of the days when clan chiefs held festivities for their clansmen. The largest offer massed pipe bands, refreshment marquees, and – these days – even funfairs. But smaller events are still impressive.

Feats of skill and strength are the order of the day. Displays of Highland dancing – the fling, jig and that most dangerous and skilful of pastimes, dancing over two crossed swords – amuse and amaze the crowds. Contestants in the Tug-o-War are loudly encouraged by their supporters, while the Hammer Throw certainly sorts out the men from the boys!

(There are two weights of hammer: 16 pounds and 22 pounds.) Putting the Stone (the Scottish version of the shot-put, with the stone weighing in at either 17 or 26 pounds) is another trial of strength, but probably the best known event is Tossing the Caber.

The Caber is a straight tree trunk between 15 and 19 feet in length and weighing 90–135 pounds – much like a telegraph pole. In fact, when telegraph poles started being erected in Scotland, they kept disappearing: it was some time before the engineers discovered they were being "borrowed" to be used as Cabers! The aim is to take a short run-up and toss the Caber forwards so that it topples over on its end. It takes considerable strength and not a little skill, and successful tosses are much less common than failures!

The Water of Life

Once considered the poor man's drink, the golden fire of fine Scotch whisky is now known and enjoyed throughout the world.

The name comes from the Gaelic "uisge beatha" or "water of life": although the main ingredient of all whisky is malted barley, other factors, such as the peat in the spring-water, contribute to the distinctive taste of different brands.

Malt whisky is usually left to mature for seven, ten, twelve or even twenty-one years (the price of a bottle reflects the length of time!): blended whisky can be much younger.

Probably the best-selling malt in the world is Glenfiddich – from the Gaelic "Glen of the Deer." In Scotland, Glen-morangie ("Glen of Great Tranquility" – the name is pronounced "glen MOR anjee") is the favorite.

Allan o' Malt

When he was young and clad in green,
With hair that covered his eyes so keen,
Baith women and men treated him mean
When on yon hills he grew sae free
Why should not Allan honoured be?

His foster father feared the worst
When Allan's head was fit to burst,
Ne'er a nurse he called, but first
Full fifty-five armed men called he!
Why should not Allan honoured be?

They ae rushed forth like hellish rooks
And hacked him wi' their claw-like hooks
Their plans they'd laid and none mistook
To bind him in a cradle cosy.
Why should not Allan honoured be?

The greatest coward in this land
If he joined up wi' Allan's band

Though he may neither go nor stand
Yet forty would nae make him flee!
Why should not Allan honoured be?

My master Allan's grown sae fine
Baith rich and strong yet e'er benign
While on men's faces he sets his sign
A nose as red as blood to see!
Why should not Allan honoured be?

My master Allan I may sore curse
He leaves me nae money in my purse
For at his call I will disburse
More than the half of my workman's fee.
Why should not Allan honoured be?

And last, of Allan to conclude,
He is well meaning, courteous and good,
And serves us well wi' daily food
And best wi' liberality!
Why should not Allan honoured be?

Midsummer Dreaming

~

The summer solstice has always had a special place in the hearts of humankind, and this is especially so in Scotland, where the bitter weather of the cold months can make the Dark Year seem endless . . .

Many of the May Day customs are happily repeated on Midsummer's Eve – couples will climb the nearest high place, and sit up all night to watch the sun rise on Midsummer's Day and make wishes for future health and happiness.

Bonfires are lit, partly as a symbolic farewell to the sun as he starts his journey into the Dark Year, and partly as a reminder to him to return in the spring!

But Midsummer is essentially a time for lovers. Young people wishing to capture the heart of their beloved would make their way to their local healing well or stream, where they would toss in a silver coin while making a wish – and sometimes attach a few hairs plucked from their head to remind the spirit of the place not to forget them!

Or they would visit a standing stone and circle it three times sunwise while concentrating on the image of the loved one (a monolith with a hole in it would be particularly lucky for young women). It was widely believed that romantic dreams seen on this night were bound to come true. Midsummer spells were particularly potent.

In the Orkney and Shetland islands, Midsummer marks the principal occasion when the selkies shed their seal-skins and dance the night away. Brave young men may have more success in gaining a selkie bride on this night, as the magic of the moment often makes the fair ones a little careless . . .

Traditional Folk Prayers

Sun

Greeting to you,
Sun of the Seasons,
As you travel the skies on high!
With your strong steps
On the wings of the height,
You are the mother of stars . . .

Sinking down into the perilous ocean,
Unharmed and unhurt,
You rise again on the quiet wave
Like a young queen in flower.

Moon

Greeting to you, New Moon,
Kindly jewel of guidance!
To you I offer my love.

Greeting to you, New Moon,
Darling of my love!
I raise my hands to you, darling of graces.

You journey on your course,
You steer the flood-tides,
You light up your face for us,
New Moon of the seasons.

Queen of guidance, queen of good-luck,
Queen of my love, New Moon of the
    seasons!

First Fruits

In ancient times, Lughnassadh (1 August; also called Lammas – "loaf-mass") celebrated the harvest that Lugh (a name for the sun god) had persuaded from the fertile earth, and the first fruits of the harvest were believed to be particularly blessed. Small loaves (bannocks) were cooked from the first grain to be harvested: these had to be baked in a fire made from rowan wood, for protection.

The head of the household handed them to each member of the family to be eaten with much ceremony, after which they all circled the fire sunwise, singing the sun's praises.

Lughnassadh was also the time for rounding up the grazing flocks and herds for inspection or sale at one of the sheep or cattle fairs. These were often an excuse for festivity, and were accompanied by much gaiety!

Corn Riggs

It was upon a Lammas night
When corn riggs are bonnie,
Beneath the moon's unclouded light
I hied away to Annie;
The time flew by, wi' careless heed,
Till 'tween the late and early;
Wi' sma' persuasion she agreed
To see me through the barley.

The sky was blue, the wind was still,
The moon was shining clearly;
I laid her down, wi' right good will,
Among the riggs o' barley:
I knew her heart was all my ain;
I lov'd her most sincerely;
I kissed her over and over again,
Among the riggs of barley.

I lock'd her in my fond embrace;
Her heart was beating rarely:

My blessings on that happy place,
Among the riggs o' barley!
But by the moon and stars so bright,
That shone that night so clearly!
She'll ever bless that happy night,
Among the riggs o' barley.

I hae been blythe wi' comrades dear;
I hae been merry drinking;
I hae been joyful gath'rin gear;
I hae been happy thinking:
But all the pleasures e'er I saw,
Though three times doubl'd fairly,
That happy night was worth them all,
Among the riggs o' barley.

Corn riggs, an' barley riggs,
And corn riggs are bonnie,
I'll ne'er forget that happy night
Among the riggs wi' Annie.

Robert Burns

The Burry Man

~

In early August, during the Ferry Fair at Queensferry, not far from Edinburgh, a strange figure can be seen – covered from head to foot with the prickly seeds of the Burdock plant . . .

Carrying a flowery staff in each hand, the Burry Man is led through the town by his two assistants – and followed by children – collecting money as he goes. On completion of his parade, he is expelled from the town.

The curious custom is believed to represent the cleansing of the community from its misdeeds and crimes, with the Burry Man acting as a kind of scapegoat – and indeed, the burred costume he wears is extremely hot and uncomfortable enough to symbolize a whole heap of sins!

Presumably also, the money helps to "pay off" the sins of the giver.

The Maiden of the Corn

~

In the age before machines, when farmers reaped fields of cereal crops with razor-sharp scythes, a natural excitement would grow as the work neared its climax.

When a whole year's work was practically over and virtually the whole harvest was safely gathered, there remained one solemn, precious moment that united the clan.

Throughout the cutting of the crop, the spirit of the corn had fled from field to field as the men worked inexorably through them. Now she was trapped in just one quivering stand of corn, surrounded by her pursuers.

It is, though, with reverence that the final blade falls, severing her from the earth. With heartfelt gratitude the chief catches the slender bundle in his hand before she drops to the ground. And it is with joy that he holds her aloft as he approaches the bonniest lass there gathered – and gives the Maiden of the Corn into her care.

The pipers and fiddlers strike up a merry tune as the Maiden is quickly bedecked with bright-colored ribbons, and paraded around for all to see. With music and dancing to banish all weariness, the procession leaves the field and heads homeward for an evening of high festivity.

The slim sheath of wheat is taken by the women and painstakingly worked into a beautiful corn dolly, and lovingly dressed as befits a queen. Then the Maiden and the lasses who prepared her are presented to the company of men assembled at the feast and toasted with cheers and whisky. She is raised high in the beams where she will preside over the year ahead. Long and joyful are the celebrations that attend the safe home-coming of the Maiden of the Corn!

Hallowe'en

Samhain (pronounced "SAH-wen") has always been a perilous time of year, when the barriers between the human world, the world of the dead, and the Otherworld of the Fey-Folk grow thin . . .

31 October marks the start of the Dark Year. In many places Samhain was actually treated as the New Year, with similar celebrations to Hogmanay but rather more solemnity and without quite so much good cheer: after all, the hard times of winter were on their way.

Houses were cleaned from top to bottom, and all washing, disposing of rubbish, and other odd jobs had to be completed before sundown. A large fire was kindled in the hearth, to ensure – symbolically – that the family would not lack heat and light through the winter. And it was important to throw a silver coin into the house through the front door as the first act on 1 November. The coin had to remain where it fell – or hidden under the carpet or rug – to make sure that sufficient money would come through the door throughout the coming year.

In ancient times there was also a great feast: surplus animals or those too sickly to survive the coming cold were slaughtered, and while most were salted or dried to provide winter supplies, the rest were cooked and eaten.

On this night the ghosts of the dead, as well as members of the Fey-Folk, could be encountered, and it was important to treat everyone with courtesy – especially strangers who might be visitors from the Otherworld, and woe betide the man or woman who offended such a visitant!

The Ghost-Knight of Hallowe'en

~

"O welcome Sir Roland!" said Margaret,
"Welcome to my secret bower.
We'll feast tonight and tomorrow be wed,
And there's nae one else in this tower."

"This nicht is Hallowe'en," said he.
"And it's drearie that I've dreamed,
That ye would slay me here and now . . .?"
And aye she did as she'd schemed.

She fled the bower all rank wi blood,
On her faithful lover's ain steed,
She spurred it into the haunted nicht
Making distance wi all speed.

Then she spied a tall young man
Upon a mount as black as jet,
Though slowly he did ride ahead
Nae closer did she get.

She whipped her steed and spurred it sore
Til his breast was in a foam
But nearer to that unhurried knight
She found she could nae come.

They plunged in at a river ford
Wi' moonlicht silver dyed,
But ever deeper the water grew
The river seemed more wide.

"O this is Hallow Morn," he cried.
"Your bridal day to be,
And the bride must ride more deeply yet
Who rides this ford wi' me!

"Ride on, ride on, proud Margaret
Til water flows o'er your brow:
For ye hae slain a faithful knight
Whose ghost claims his bride here and
    now!"

The Roaring Game

Curling is a uniquely Scottish sport. While not strictly a festival, cold, bright winter weather often tempts groups of Scots out onto the frozen lochs to challenge each other at the "roaring game," so called for the loud hum the curling stones make as they glide across the ice!

The stones themselves are large, one-handled, well-polished, flattened granite spheres that are thrown carefully across the ice. Once the stone is in motion it must not be touched, but the ice before it can be smoothed by brushing with a broom.

Once in a while, when the weather is particularly favorable, there is a "Grand Match," with North Scotland playing against South Scotland. Hundreds of people attend such matches — but the fun appears to be much more important than the outcome of the game!

Christmas

Yule – the winter solstice, celebrated around 21 December with bonfires, relief that the Dark Year was halfway through, and a feast – was later expropriated into the Christian religion, moved to 25 December and called Christmas.

Christmas customs in Scotland don't vary greatly from any other country, although the welcome warmth, good eating and gift-giving that accompanies the festival may be appreciated more here than in warmer climes! And the Christmas tree is treated with particular reverence, as a symbol that no matter how cold and bitter the winter, there is still life in the earth, just waiting for the sun's reappearance in the spring . . .

One custom that was perhaps more prevalent in Scotland than elsewhere was the placing of silver charms into the Christmas pudding. Traditionally these were designed to tell your fortune: the sixpence coin symbolized wealth, the ring marriage, the wishbone good luck, the thimble work. Of course, others could be included as desired – perhaps a heart for love, a cradle for a new baby, a boat for a long journey . . .

Scotland has a different version of the well-known Christmas song "The Twelve Days of Christmas" (the verses being chanted by successive members of the family), although it appears it isn't sung very often these days:

"The king sent his lady on the first Yule day,
A popingo-aye:
Who learns my carol and carries it away?"

(A popingo-aye is a parrot.)

"The king sent to his lady on the second Yule day,

Three partridges: a popingo-aye;
Who learns my carol and carries it away?

The king sent to his lady on the third Yule
day,
Three plovers; three partridges; a
popingo-aye;
Who learns my carol and carries it away?

The king sent to his lady on the fourth
Yule day,
A goose that was grey; three plovers; (etc)
Who learns my carol and carries it away?

The king sent to his lady on the fifth Yule
day,
Three starlings; a goose that was gray;
(etc)
Who learns my carol and carries it away?

The king sent to his lady on the sixth Yule
day,
Three goldspinks; three starlings; (etc)
Who learns my carol and carries it away?

The king sent to his lady on the seventh
   Yule day,
A bull that was brown; three goldspinks;
   (etc)
Who learns (etc)."

The remaining verses contain –

Three ducks a-merry laying;
Three swans a-merry swimming;
An Arabian baboon;
Three hinds a-merry hunting;
Three maids a-merry dancing;
Three stalks o' merry corn.

RITES OF PASSAGE

Birth

∾

The act of being born is the first, and of course the most important, rite of passage we ever undertake: without birth there can be nothing else.

Childbirth is surrounded by mystery and peril. The expectant woman becomes an object of considerable awe, often hidden away so that evil cannot find her and possibly infect the unborn babe — and also so that she cannot use the mysterious power she possesses at this time to cause harm to others. Midwives have special abilities of their own, making them party to the new mother's power rather than endangered by it.

Even after the child is born there may still be danger, and a number of protective methods exist to ensure its safe-keeping until it can be named.

The Blessing of Fire

～

Even today, in a world of antibiotics, immunizations, genetic engineering, and human intervention into the most abstruse areas of knowledge, fire is still seen as the great purifier. Without the fire of the sun there would be no life, without the hearthfire there could be no clan, without the alchemical Element of Fire there could be no light to lighten our darkness – and the faithful would argue that without the light of religion human lives would be dark indeed . . .

Whatever the individual belief, fire in its numerous forms has always been seen as sacred. Fearful, unpredictable and whimsical, yes, but still sacred.

The period after a child has been born, and before it has been officially named – either presented to the tribe and named according to the old practices, baptized into the Christian faith, or whatever – is always a perilous time. In Christian tradition, the infant's soul may easily be taken into custody by the Devil. In the Old Tradition, the child is at risk of being spirited away by malevolent members of the Fey-Folk, or of having its soul stolen so that it wastes away and dies.

To prevent such a tragedy, fire in the form of a flaming torch was carried sunwise around mother and child as soon after birth as possible, to create a barrier that fairies, witches or evil spirits could not pass. This served to protect them both against malevolent influences until the child could be named – at which time it could no longer fall prey to the unseen world.

It is said, however, that the Fey-Folk weep at such naming ceremonies, as they destroy the child's innate psychic abilities . . .

Changelings

~

Quite why the Fey-Folk would wish to steal a human child and leave one of their number in exchange has never been really discovered. There are a number of possibilities, of course: some said that the race was growing weak, and stole away humans to increase its strength; others insisted that the Fey-Folk could not bear to see the child deprived of its native psychic powers (which happened automatically at naming) and brought the child into their company to protect and nurture its abilities. Or maybe it was simply done for mischief – the Fey-Folk, especially the lesser members such as the goblins or Brownies, could be capricious, especially if they thought themselves slighted or insulted in some way.

Usually the first the mother knew was when the changeling – the fairy that replaced the human baby – began to grow suddenly thin and sickly in the cradle. Often it later transformed into an elderly member of the Fey-Folk. However, if the parents could reveal the deception before the changeling showed its true nature, the Fey-Folk were duty-bound to return their prize to its home.

To prevent the child from being stolen and a changeling left in its place, bunches of herbs, usually including rowan and garlic, were hung on the cradle's sides. Or the mother might hang an opened pair of scissors over the child – the metal would deter the thieves, as would the shape, which resembled a cross and signified the baptism the child would shortly go through. But in reality, nothing could be truly effective except giving the child its name . . .

The Witch Mother

~

Willie has travelled afar o'er the sea
And brought home a wife, his mither to see,
But for all her grace and long golden hair
And for the bairn she shortly should bear,
His mither's heart was black as pitch –
For Willie's mither is a vile rank witch.

And when his wife's full term has come
It's to his mither Willie has gone.
"Born," she cried. "That bairn shan't be,
Nor live long will your fair lady,
But she will die and turn to clay,
And another wife then ye will tae."

"My lady's goblet has a golden stem
And every colour o' precious gem,
And she has a girdle o' the good red gold
Wi' fifty silver bells around all told,
Wi' gold her steed is shod sae grand
There's none its equal in all the land,

"All these gifts they shall be thine
If ye will aid her bear our bairn!"
"Yon bairn shall ne'er see licht o' day,
And your lady will die and turn to clay."
"Mither ye are nae man's friend –
I wish my life were at an end!"

As Willie to his lady hied
A Brownie leaped up by his side
"Gae ye to yon market-place
Buy ye there a loaf o' wax
Mould it as a bairn may be
Wi' twa glass beads to see.

Invite your mither to yon kirk –
This Christ'ning she may never shirk –
Then ken all she may say and do,
Then Willie, be ye bold and true!"
And Willie swift and sure has did
The fullness of all he was bid.

His mither entered the kirk and hissed
"O woe that I should witness this!
O who has loosed the nine witch-knots
I set among that lady's locks,
And who's ta'en out the combs o' care
I set among that lady's hair,

And who has killed the master kid
That passed beneath that lady's bed
And who has untied her left shoe
To let the bairn be born? Aye, who?"
Then Willie bold and truly did
All the things his mither said –

And bought the bairn safe to licht o' day,
And saved his lady from Death's cold sway!

Babies

~

Being born feet first bestows special healing powers, particularly the ability to cure sleepwalking. The virtue resides in the feet themselves, which need to be applied directly to the afflicted part, skin to skin (for example, by carefully standing on the sleepwalker's bare feet nine times in succession).

When a babe is born with a caul protecting its head, the hallihoo or "holy hood" is carefully removed and kept safely hidden away. Should it be destroyed, the bairn will pine and perish. Such a child, however, will have Second Sight, and is safe from the powers of sorcerers.

Cauls were also used as a charm offering protection against immersion in salt water. They were frequently placed aboard vessels of all descriptions, in order to avert the perils of shipwreck.

Aiken Drum
(Scottish Children's Rhyme)

~

There was a man lived in the moon,
Lived in the moon, lived in the moon,
There was a man lived in the moon
And his name was Aiken Drum.

And he played upon a ladle,
A ladle, a ladle,
And he played upon a ladle
And his name was Aiken Drum.

He made his hat o' curds an' whey (etc)

He made his coat o' dark roast beef (etc)

He made his buttons o' penny loaves (etc)

He made his waiskit o' bridie crust (etc)

He made his breeks o' haggis bags (etc)

There was another man lived in the moon
Lived in the moon, lived in the moon,
There was another man lived in the moon
And his name was Willy Wood.

And he played upon a razor,
A razor, a razor,
And he played upon a razor
And his name was Willy Wood.

And he ate up all the curds an' whey (etc)

And he ate up all the dark roast beef (etc)

And he ate up all the penny loaves (etc)

And he ate up all the bridie crust (etc)

But he choked upon the haggis bags
Haggis bags, haggis bags,
But he choked upon the haggis bags
And that stopped Willy Wood!

A Few Proverbs

Only a fool weds at Yule,
For when harvest is ripe for reaping
The bairn is set for bearing!

Whoe'er to the north and south sets his bed,
male offspring shall surely beget.

Tae ease the labour and pain
O' bearing a bonny bairn,
Open every household lock
And loose each garment's knot.

The Good Wee Wife
(A Scottish Nursery Rhyme)

There was a wee wifie tossed up in a blanket
Ninety-nine times as high as the moon.

And what she did there I canna declare
But in her basket she carried the sun.

"Wee wifie, wee wifie, wee wifie," quoth I
"Oh what are ye doing up there sae high?"

"I'm blowing the cold clouds out of the sky!"
"Well done, well done, well done!" Quoth I.

RITES OF PASSAGE

Love, Courtship & Marriage

~

Between birth and death come all the pleasures
of life – and the greatest of these is love!

> "... were I in the wildest waste,
> Sae black and bare, sae black and bare,
> The desert were a Paradise,
> If thou wert there, if thou wert there.
> Or were I monarch of the globe,
> Wi' thee to reign, wi' thee to reign,
> The brightest jewel in my crown
> Would be my queen, would be my queen."
>
> Robert Burns,
> "O, Wert Thou in the Cauld Blast"

A Red, Red Rose

O, my love is like a red, red rose,
That's newly sprung in June.
O my love is like the melody,
That's sweetly play'd in tune.

As fair art thou, my bonny lass,
So deep in love am I,
And I will love thee still my dear,
Til all the seas run dry.

Til all the seas run dry, my dear,
And the rocks melt wi' the sun!
And I will love thee still, my dear,
While the sands o' life shall run.

And fare thee well, my only love,
And fare thee well a while!
And I will come again, my love,
Though it were ten thousand mile!

Robert Burns

Clairvoyance

~

To dream of a future husband place a piece of wedding cake beneath your pillow, along with a list of three prospective lovers. To dream of any one of them is a sign that he will become your "significant other"!

Another charm to identify a spouse is to spot the thin, first crescent of the new moon, and say:

> "New Moon, true Moon, tell tae me
> If . . . my ain true love will be:
> If he will marry me in haste
> Show tae me his bonny face,
> If he will marry me betide
> Show tae me see his bonny side,
> If he will never marry me
> Let me see the back o' he."

Charm of the Garter

~

At Hallowe'en a maid may see her future husband in a dream.

She needs only take the garter she has worn all day on her left leg, and sleep with it under her pillow. But before she tucks it away she must secretly tie three knots in it, saying as she ties each one –

"This knot, this knot I knit
To see the thing I ne'er saw yet,
To see my love in his array
And where he spends his every day
And what his occupation be
This night in my sleep I'll see.

"And if my love be clad in green
His love for me may not be keen,
And if my love be clad in grey
His love for me is far away,
But if my love be clad in blue
His love for me is very true!"

Engagement Ring

~

A newly engaged lass may show off her ring to her friends, but no one else must wear it past their second knuckle, or bad luck will follow – the wedding might not take place, or, even worse, the lad might fall for another!

Once carefully positioned on the other's finger, however, the friend may twirl it thrice round toward her heart, all the time wishing for a man of her own.

In returning the ring to its owner, special care needs be taken to avoid saying "thank you" for this will void the magic. Instead the friend may wish the bride-to-be "good luck," and she in turn may say "I hope your wish comes true."

Courtship Charm

~

To turn a man's heart toward you, take a pinch of salt and cast it into an open fire on three Friday nights in succession. Each time say:

> "It is not this salt I wish to burn
> But I wish my lover's heart to turn
> That neither rested nor happy he may
> be
> Til he comes hither to speak to me."

A bonnie lass is soon a bride.

~

The livelier the mischief
The merrier the sport!

Bonnie lasses wear no purses.

~

A wooed lass that laughs is half way won!

~

A dowerless dame sits lang at hame.

~

Better a fortune in a wife
Than with a wife!

~

A man may woo where he will –
But will wed always where his hopes lie . . .

Lord Lovel

Lord Lovel stands at his stable-door
Sat on his milk white steed,
His Lady Nanciebel chances by,
And bids her Lord good speed.

"O where are ye going, my beloved Lord?"
"O I am going on a far journey,
But I'll return in seven years
When many wonders have I seen."

When he was gone a year away,
A year but barely one,
A dark fancy quenched his wanderlust –
That Nanciebel was gone.

Straight home he turned and swiftly rode,
And when he entered the town
He heard at once the tolling bell,
And dismal grew his frown.

"For who now rings this passing bell?"
– They said "For Lady Nanciebel
Who died, forlorn, of a broken heart –
Quite forgot by her Lord Lovel."

In the kirk he lifts the coffin lid up,
And the linen shroud folds down,
And when once he kissed her pale, pale
    lips
All his tears came tumbling down.

And where she lies dead from purest love
Lord Lovel now dies of sorrow:
From out their graves, together at last,
Twa sweet briar roses grow.

They climb together the tall church tower
And when they can grow no higher
There they entwine in a true lovers' knot
For all lovers true to admire.

Gretna Green

Just over the border with England, in Dumfries and Galloway, is the Old Blacksmith's House, the first house in the village of Gretna Green – renowned the world over for its romantic tales of eloping young lovers . . .

In the days when the age of consent for marriage was twenty-one, Scottish Law permitted young couples to be married, without their parents' consent, from the age of sixteen. All that was required for the marriage to be made legal was for both parties to declare their wish and intent to be married before an official – such as a blacksmith – and two other witnesses.

Instead of an altar, the blacksmith's forge was used, and naturally such weddings were very popular amongst the rebellious young, especially in the days when parental discipline was often very harsh and uncom-promising: news of the "anvil marriages" spread fast!

Such weddings continued until 1940, when they were halted by an Act of Parliament. Nevertheless, the name "Gretna Green" still holds a fascination of its own – and there is something very satisfying, given the great good luck associated with the horseshoe, in the idea of having a marriage union sanctified by the man who actually makes them!

A Few Superstitions

~

It is a grave miscalculation to wed when the moon is waning, since the couple's prospects of joy will be waning with the moon. A wedding during the waxing moon, however, foretells an increase in good fortune, and a wedding timed for the fullness of the moon ensures a prosperous and delightful future for the happy couple.

~

Other factors influencing the choice of the wedding day are the avoidance of Friday (traditionally the unluckiest day of the week due to its association with Christ's death), and the custom that a bride who marries after sunset is doomed to a tragic life – including seeing the death of her children, and going to an early grave herself . . .

And lastly, avoid being married in May, for:

Marry in May, rue for aye
For the bairns'll die of a decay.

The Twa Sisters: a Tale of Jealousy

~

There were twa sisters lived in a bower
(Binnorie, O Binnorie;)

There came a knight to be their wooer
(By the bonnie mill-dams o' Binnorie.)

He courted the eldest wi' brooch and rings,
(Binnorie, O Binnorie;)
But he loved the youngest above a' things.

The sisters were waiting on the river bank
Where their father's ship would come tae
land.

The eldest to her sister turned
And grabbed and pitched her into the
waves.

"Help me and I'll give ye half my land!"
"Nae, but I'll have all thy land."

"Help me and William shall be thy love!"
"Nae, but he shall be sure enough.

Your cherry cheeks and flaxen hair
Shall outshine mine nae mair!"

Sometimes she sank and sometimes she
    swam,
Til she came to Binnorie mill-dam.

A harper found her corpse there alone
And a harp he made from her breast bone.

He stringed it wi' her flaxen hair,
Whose doleful notes were hard tae bear.

He brought the harp tae her father's hall
And there was the court assembled all.

He set the harp down on a stone
And there it began tae play alone.

"Woe tae my false sister Helen," it sang
"Whose envy did me deadly wrong!"

When Green should Ne'er be Seen

The color green is traditionally associated with the Fey-Folk and all things unearthly, and is taboo at weddings:

> They that marry in green
> Their sorrow is soon seen.

This prohibition against the bride and groom marrying in green clothing has, on occasion, been taken to such extremes that even green vegetables have been banned from the wedding feast – a tradition that would indulge the taste of many a young bridesmaid!

Coming and Going

~

Even though it might mean walking in a circle around the outside of her house, or even taking a long and round-about route, the bride should always start out on her procession to the marriage ceremony by turning to her right.

Moreover, during the journey she must not turn and look back lest bad luck follow her down the aisle!

Tossing a confetti of wheat grains over the newlyweds showers them with wishes of prosperity. Tying old boots and shoes to the back of their carriage expresses the hope that they will be blessed with many bonny bairns!

It is unlucky for newlyweds to return home by the same route that they (or either one of them) took to get to the wedding. To do so tempts fate to return them to an unmarried state . . .

More Words of Wisdom

~

When all are bonnie lasses,
Whence come the bad wives?

~

A maiden should be coy and sweet –
But a wife may burn kirks!

~

Ye may beat the Devil intae a wife,
But ye'll never beat him out o' her!

~

If the laird slight his wife,
Sae shall all the kitchen staff.

~

A penny-weight of love
Is worth a pound of law.

RITES OF PASSAGE

The Final Rite of Passage

~

Death is the great leveler – and the circumstances surrounding it can be fraught with danger both physical, psychological, and spiritual.

    A number of precautions must be taken to aid the spirit of the departed to pass safely and peacefully into the afterlife . . .

> Weep for the first in a new burial plot
> For that body falls tae the Devil's lot.
> The last to be buried in an old kirk yard
> Til doomsday will be its watch and guard.
>
> Time and thinking tame the strongest
>   grief . . .

A Farewell to the Loved One

~

There are several variants to the well-known and well-loved song, Loch Lomond. One story of its origin (there are several) says that it was penned by a Scottish soldier captured by the English during the Battle of Culloden (16 April 1746). Certain that he would be hanged, he wrote it as a farewell to his beloved. She herself is said to have been gifted (or cursed) with Second Sight, and met with him in spirit before he died. They promised to be true to each other, and to meet again in the afterlife. The "low road" of the song is the road of death . . .

By yon bonnie banks and by yon bonnie braes
Where the sun shines bright on Loch
    Lomond,
Me and my true love spent many a day,
Hand in hand as we roamed o'er the heather.

You'll take the high road and I'll take the low
    road,
And I'll be in Scotland before you,
For me and my true love will never meet
    again
On the bonnie, bonnie banks of Loch
    Lomond.

T'was there that we parted, in yon shady glen,
On the steep sides of Ben Lomond,
But the broken heart knows no second
    spring,
And it's there you must weep while we're
    parted.

I'll take the high road and you'll take the low
    road,
And I'll stay in Scotland and await you,
And me and my true love will yet meet again,
Far above the bonnie banks of Loch
    Lomond . . .

The Green Lady and the Washer at the Ford

~

In the Highlands the eerie wailing of the Green Lady can be heard, heralding an approaching death . . .

The Green Lady is kin to the Irish Bean Sidh (Banshee), the spirit of a supernaturally gifted ancestress who watches over the family. She cannot interfere directly in its affairs, but she is able to warn of forthcoming calamities, such as death, by crying aloud in the night, and so forewarn the household in her care.

A much less welcome figure is the Washer at the Ford, a frightening figure who haunts the burns and rills of the Highlands. She most often appears as an ugly hag washing blood-stained clothing in a stream, and to encounter her betokens your own imminent death. A good reason for staying home, perhaps?

A Few Superstitions

~

When someone dies at home all the windows in the house should be opened so that the soul might the more easily depart.

As close to the moment of death as is practicable, every clock in the house should be stopped, so that time can stand still until the corpse leaves on its final journey to the graveyard . . .

Between the death and the funeral it is customary to cover every mirror in the house where the body lies, with white cloths. This is to protect the mourners from the risk that the image of the deceased might be seen staring out from behind them – such a sight is an ill omen indeed!

Sometimes this precaution is extended to include all shiny objects that could cast such reflections, such as ornaments or pots and pans.

The corpse should never be left unattended while it lies in state in its earthly home. Even throughout the long dark nights a watch or "wake" is held – often with much noise, the playing of practical jokes, and an abundance of ribald merriment! The brighter and livelier the wake the better, for the more heartily it is celebrated the higher the honor and respect that is accorded to the deceased . . .

Traditionally, in the Highlands it was customary for the funeral to be a signal for relatives to break into high-spirited and traditionally bloody fighting!

Once a corpse has been laid out, great care is needed to ensure no tear falls upon it, lest the spirit be touched with mortal attachments and remain earthbound.

It is just as important, however, for each member of the household, friends and family to touch the deceased in fond farewell.

A funeral procession seen through a window is an omen of great misfortune, but this doom can be lifted by going outdoors so that the sky is above your head, and watching the procession pass away.

To prevent victims of murder from stalking the earth bewailing their fate, take the shoes from their feet and have them buried in beach sand below the high tide line.

When the bodies of strangers who had been drowned at sea were washed up on the beach, they were traditionally interred on the shore where they were found, in a grave dug carefully between the high and low water marks. Otherwise their ghosts might return to haunt the living . . .

Young Benjie

Young Marjorie and Benjie's love
Waxed too strong to restrain,
So all the more, when they fell out,
The darker was their pain.

With bitter heart, by pale moonlight
He's gone to Marjorie's home
She's gone hersel' to ope the door
For this night she's alone.

So soft she smiled and bowed to him –
"My heart's nae hard as rock . . ."
But up he took her in his arms
And drowned her in yon loch!

Her kin have taken up the corpse
And laid it on the ground –
"O who has killed dear Marjorie
And how can he be found?"

That night it was her low lykewake,
Next morn her burial day,
And they'd keep vigil with doors ajar
To hear what she may say.

About the dead hour o' the nicht
The cocks began to crow
And in the glower o' candle licht
The corpse writhed and gasped low –

"Cut out Benjie's twa grey eyes,
"That looked on me sae long,
"And tie a green scarf 'round the neck
O' that man who did me wrong!

And ay, at every seven years' end
He must come back tae see yon loch
For that's the penance he maun do
Til his tears may melt a rock . . ."

The Twa Corbies

There were twa ravens on a yew tree,
Mickle and black as night may be,
And one unto the other did say
"O whar'll we gang and dine today?
Shall we fly to the wild salt sea
Or swoop beneath the greenwood tree?"

"As I sat on the salt sea strand
I spied a ship draw nigh tae land,
I shook my wings and tossed my beak
Sae that ship sank wi' many a shriek!
On the sand they lie – ane, twa, three –
I shall feed by the wild salt sea."

"Come, I will show ye a sweeter sight,
A lonesome glen, and a new slain knight;
His blood yet on the grass is hot,
His sword half drawn, his arrows unshot,
And no one kens that he lies there
But his hawk, his hound and his lady fair."

His hound is to the hunting gone,
His hawk to fetch the wild-fowl home,
His lady's away with another mate,
So we shall make our dinner sweet;
Our banquet's sure, our feasting free,
Come and dine 'neath the greenwood tree.

Ye shall sit on his white neck bane;
I will pluck out his bonny blue een;
Ye'll take a tress o' his yellow hair
To thatch your nest when it gets bare;
The golden down on his young chin
Will do to bed my young ones in!"

"O cauld and bare his bed will be
When winter's storms sing in the tree,
A turf at his head, a stone at his feet,
He'll nae hear the maidens sigh and weep,
O'er his white banes the birds shall fly
The wild deer bound, and foxes cry!"

...GHOULIES AND GHOSTIES...

~

Scotland is rich in ghosts and has haunted sites aplenty — castles, houses, wild places, even an aerodrome!

The following pages detail some of the best known, as well as some less familiar eerie locales — in case you should find yourself in the area and decide to try your hand at psychic detective...

PLEASE NOTE: Not all of the following sites are open to the public. Please ensure that you respect the privacy and personal wishes of the inhabitants — human as well as ghostly!

The Pretty Ghost of Allanbank

~

The patter of high-heeled shoes, the rustle of a silk dress trimmed with pearling lace, means pretty Pearlin' Jean is near . . .

Sir Robert Stuart of Allanbank, which stood on the banks of the Blackadder river, once loved a young French Sister of Charity by the name of Jean. After a little time he tired of her and returned home to Scotland to marry one of his own people.

No one would have been surprised if Jean had given in to despair: her vocation lost, her honor surrendered, her heart broken. But the girl was made of stronger stuff.

She followed him home, and confronted her erstwhile lover and his betrothed as they were about to leave for a drive. Afraid that his wife-to-be would turn from him – and perhaps also to rid himself of what he may have seen as a potential blackmailer,

Sir Robert bade the driver move on – and Jean was crushed to death under his carriage wheels.

But even in death she proved tenacious. Her blood-spattered ghostly form became such a regular visitor that the household – with the exception of Sir Robert and his wife – became quite used to her: it may even be said they considered her a part of the family!

Over the centuries several attempts were made to exorcize her, but she resisted them all, continuing to haunt the family whose ancestor had caused her dishonor and death. Well, you know what they say about "a woman scorned"!

The Ghostly Piper of Duntrune Castle

~

The magnificent twelfth-century castle, standing proudly in a slight rise on the shores of Loch Crinan was, until 1729, the home of the Campbells of Duntrune – except, that is, for one brief spell in the early seventeenth century when the MacDonalds captured the castle. It was shortly thereafter recaptured by the Campbells, who killed everyone but the MacDonald's piper: a half-superstitious act, for pipers have occupied a privileged position throughout the centuries, and to harm one might cause great bad luck . . .

Some time later the MacDonald Coll Ciotach ravaged northwards from Kintyre, intent on obliterating everything Campbell in revenge. The piper, seeing his master's clansman approaching and intent on alerting him to the strong Campbell defense, played the traditional pibroch "The Piper's

Warning to his Master" on his bagpipes. The warning was successful and Coll Ciotach turned back, but the Campbells, furious at being cheated of a battle, cut off the piper's fingers . . .

It is said that he bled slowly to death, and for centuries afterwards the haunting sound of the pibroch echoed eerily through the castle. Then, in the early part of the twentieth century, a fingerless skeleton was found bricked up in one of the walls.

The remains were given an Episcopalian burial, but some years later the music began again, now accompanied by inexplicable noises, pictures falling from walls, and heavy objects moving of their own accord. It has been suggested that the piper, who would most likely have been a Catholic, is uncomfortable at being buried in the wrong church . . .

The Homely Hauntings at Ballachulish House

~

It was in the ancient home of the Stewarts of Ballachulish that Captain Robert Campbell received the order that led to the massacre of the MacDonalds at Glencoe . . .

Although the house and the Stewarts had nothing more to do with the massacre, it would be surprising if a building so close to a scene of such tragedy did not have at least some supernatural apparitions attached to it!

Such is indeed the case – and the apparitions all seem to be concerned with the day-to-day running of an ancient house. A ghostly Scotsman mounted on a horse is often seen – and heard! – galloping up to the main door, dismounting and entering the house – then disappearing. His identity is not certain, but it has been suggested that he is a member of the Stewart clan, or possibly a messenger still intent on delivering his news, even though the recipients are now long dead.

The faint clatter of metal pots and pans clinking together marks the presence of a ghostly tinker, who haunts the area around the house, still trying to ply his trade even in death.

Within the house, the ghost of a little old lady (reputedly the mother of a previous owner) flits busily from room to room, keeping an eye on the family and making sure that everything in the household is in proper order.

Another ghost, whose sudden and unexpected appearances cause consternation, walks through walls in the house; no one has ever recognized the shadowy figure.

In recent years there have also been strange and unaccountable smells and mysterious knocking sounds – maybe a plumber has joined the ghostly host!

Ballechin House

~

Although the main house no longer exists, the area where it stood is still, reputedly, haunted by the phantom Black Dog of Ballechin House . . .

The estate, near Aberfeldy, was the home of the Steuarts, an old and well-respected family. Following his retirement, Major Robert Steuart lived here around 1873, with 27-year-old Sarah, a farmer's daughter, as housekeeper. As well as being slightly crippled – he limped from the effects of an old wound – the Major was known to be somewhat eccentric: he had often said that after his death he was determined to reappear in the shape of a black dog! His unconventionality may have passed without undue notice, were it not for young Sarah falling ill and dying within three days.

There is of course no proof whatsoever

that the Major had anything to do with her death, but the gossip started and the house was shunned by its neighbors. The Major became something of a recluse, and when he died the house passed to his nephew – who immediately had all fourteen dogs on the estate shot dead.

Then the hauntings started. The sound of limping footsteps echoed in the corridors, screams and cries drifted through the air from distant rooms, a ghostly black dog was seen prowling the estate and heard flinging itself against the main door. The figure of a nun – reputedly Isabella, Robert Steuart's sister – was glimpsed, weeping over her brother's fate, and the sound of voices came from empty rooms.

Even today, sensitive people can feel an unsettling atmosphere around the place, but it is eerie rather than evil.

The Red Fox of Barcaldine House

~

Not an animal, but a man – Colin Campbell of Glenure, who was murdered by a sniper in 1756. He lay in state at Barcaldine House before his internment at Ardchatton Priory, and his ghost (in full Highland dress) is now often met in the small glen near the house, following the people who walk there . . .

It may be a particularly troubled ghost. The man accused of Campbell's murder, a Stewart, was hanged at Ballachulish, but it was later discovered that he was innocent of the crime – the true murderer was never found. While no guilt could possibly attach itself to the unfortunate Campbell himself, the miscarriage of justice may well have been keenly felt by the ghost. However, it is more likely that his restlessness is caused by his murder having never been properly avenged.

There is a second ghost at the house, a

lovely lady dressed in blue. no one is sure of her identity, but she seems to love music. Although she is also sometimes to be found walking in the glen, she is most often seen in the house – and there is always music playing when she appears.

Could she be an ancient Campbell whose love of music and dancing has led her to remain on earth, so as to be near the source of her greatest pleasure? Or perhaps the music reminds her of her lost lover, killed in battle or lost overseas? We may never be able to do more than guess.

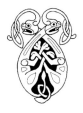

The Ghostly Deer of Arran

~

Brodick Castle on the Isle of Arran has an ancient pedigree. The red castle stands on the site of a Viking fortress, and parts of the building date from the fourteenth century. As might be expected of such a place, the stronghold boasts several ghosts.

The most benign is that of a gentleman, usually encountered in the library, reading or deep in meditation, wearing a long green jacket and breeches and a powdered wig. No one is certain who he is, but he seems to be a man of some learning with a love of study. Perhaps he stays to read the books he had no time to peruse in life . . .

A somewhat more sinister phantom can be met on the back staircase of the castle. In 1700, during the plague, three lady visitors to the place, believed by their host to be afflicted with the deadly disease, were reputedly walled up somewhere in the stronghold to prevent the plague from affecting the other inhabitants. The ghostly Gray Lady is said to be a grisly reminder of this cruel act of self-preservation.

But probably the most ominous of all is the appearance of a solitary and beautiful white deer. White deer are associated with the Fey-Folk, sometimes as their messengers, sometimes as enchanted humans who cannot return to mortal form until a certain action has been taken. However, in the case of the Hamiltons, the hereditary owners of Brodick Castle, the white deer is surely a herald from the Otherworld: it always appears immediately before the head of the family is due to die . . .

The Haunted Bay

~

Ten miles south of Cape Wrath, on the wild and craggy northeast coast of Scotland, is the isolated sweep of Sandwood Bay, a peaceful place, if lonely . . .

The only dwelling anywhere near the beach is Sandwood Cottage, untenanted for many years – which is not entirely surprising, given that both the beach and the cottage are haunted by the ghost of an old sailor.

The ghostly man is described as being enormously tall, bearded, and dressed in eighteenth-century clothing with sea-boots, a long dark cloak, and brass buttons on his tunic. He has laid claim to all driftwood found on the beach, on one occasion appearing from thin air to shout at a pair of laborers gathering firewood, saying that the wood was his property.

Those few brave folk who have dared to

spend the night in the cottage have heard ghostly footsteps, hooves clattering over the roof, and the sound of slamming doors and windows being smashed. One visitor actually awoke to find himself being smothered by an invisible heavy mass. Come daylight, though, no natural causes for the disturbances can ever be found.

No one knows who the sailor is, but he has been seen both by local people – fishermen, crofters, shepherds – and also by many visitors. His materializations are surprisingly frequent, and he disappears as mysteriously as he appears, sometimes leaving a trail of footprints ending at the water's edge...

The Grisly Pair of Crathes Castle

~

The Lady in Green glides across the room to lift the child from beside the hearth – then both figures mysteriously fade away ...

Crathes Castle near Banchory, ancient home of the Burnetts of Leys, dates from the sixteenth century, and the Green Lady (who has been appearing to the family for at least four hundred years) often materializes just before the death of one of the Burnett family. Although her identity is unknown, it is traditionally reckoned that overweening ambition and resentment drove her to murder, and her spirit cannot rest: an appropriate phantom to appear as a herald of approaching death!

Workmen making repairs in the "haunted room" in the nineteenth century actually made the shocking discovery of the skeleton of a woman and child in the vicinity of the fireplace. It would appear that sometime at the end of the seventeenth century the daughter of the house disgraced herself and the family by becoming pregnant by her father's personal servant: the only way the family honor could be redeemed was by the dismissal of the ghillie, and the "disappearance" of the girl and the child . . .

It seems likely that the two ghosts have become confused over the years. Visitors have reported seeing the wraith of the young woman in what has become known as the Green Lady's Room for the last couple of hundred years – yet the original Green Lady is far older than that. Of course, the two are very different in character – one the pathetic victim of her own indiscretion, the other a warning of doom – but we may entertain a measure of hope that the two may find some solace in each other's company.

The Headless Lady of Drumlanrig

~

Along the corridors of the ancient stronghold of the Douglas Clan walks Lady Anne Douglas – carrying her head in her hands...

Drumlanrig Castle, near Thornhill in Dumfries and Galloway, has had something of a varied history. The original castle was built in the fourteenth century. The present – built by William Douglas, who was so horrified by the cost of construction he could only bear to spend one night there – was used as a refuge by "Bonnie" Prince Charlie in 1745.

The reason why the headless lady is reputed to be Anne Douglas has been forgotten – but the question lends itself to considerable speculation! Was she beheaded in an accident, or, perhaps more likely, murdered?

Lady Douglas is not the only ghost at the castle, however. The Haunted Room is frequented by a strange "furry creature" – sometimes described as a monkey or ape of some kind, sometimes as something more sinister, although in the main it appears benign.

The castle is also haunted by the ghost of a little girl in a long dress. She only appears to people who are seriously ill, but happily there is no record of such individuals dying after her visit!

Inverawe House

~

The gracious manor house of Inverawe, near Taynuilt in Argyllshire, is the site of one of the most intriguing hauntings in Scotland . . .

The Campbell clan have been associated with Inverawe for over four hundred years. The house was once the home of Colin Campbell, who was murdered by the "Appin Murderer." Mary, Queen of Scots visited here, and history relates she was particularly impressed by her dinner of local salmon!

Inverawe is noted for two apparitions. The first is, according to one tradition, the murdered foster brother of one Duncan Campbell, whose specter has been walking since the middle of the eighteenth century. However, another legend has it that the ghost is actually that of Duncan himself, who died of wounds earned in the attack on Ticonderoga in 1758. The "haunted" room in the house is itself known as the Ticonderoga room.

Perhaps the more interesting apparition, however – and certainly the more romantic – is that of the golden-haired young lady, known as "Green Jean," a benign ghost whose history is most intriguing . . .

Green Jean is reputed to have been in life Mary Cameron, the betrothed of a young Laird of Inverawe. She was the only survivor of an outbreak of the plague, which killed off all her family and their servants. In a bold, brave effort to save his beloved, the young laird charged to the rescue, made her bathe in the sea to wash away the infection, then installed her in a cave, away from suspicious eyes, and cared for her until she recovered.

They went on to be married and have a large family, and we can only assume that their life was a happy one.

Green Jean, perhaps as a thank-you for her narrow escape, apparently chose to remain at Inverawe after death, and has been seen by a number of Campbells over the years.

In general she is a polite and friendly ghost, graciously opening doors for people when occasion arises, although she has severely startled more than a few guests in this way over the years! Robert Ross was surprised, though apparently not frightened, to see her ghost as he was driving sheep along Inverawe Road – his sheep actually stopped to allow her to pass . . .

In 1912 new owners moved into the house, and the night before their arrival, when the house was empty of furnishings, loud and frightened screams were heard coming from the upper rooms. Apparently Green Jean was less than happy about finding her home thus bare and disarranged!

A Clean Ghost!

~

The Moncrieffe Arms Hotel, an old coaching inn not far from Perth, had a long history of hauntings. Although they were usually of the audible kind – strange noises, footsteps, the sound of weeping from upstairs – no one was able to pin down exactly which room they were coming from or offer an explanation for their cause.

However, after the Young family took over the inn in the late 1970s, Mr Young, in an episode that doesn't appear to have been repeated (yet, at any rate), went upstairs and found the bathroom locked and the noise of splashing and running water coming clearly through the door. A few minutes later he returned to find the bathroom empty – and completely dry and quite cold.

Apparently ghosts don't need to use towels!

Sad Lady Jane

~

On the banks of Loch Ardblair stands Ardblair Castle, the home of the ancient and venerable Blair family since time immemorial . . .

Both the Blairs and their neighbors the Drummonds were stout supporters of Robert the Bruce, but even with this in common the two families feuded constantly – a not uncommon situation in Scotland.

This enmity eventually led to tragedy when young Lady Jane Drummond fell hopelessly in love with a member of the rival family. Despite all the loving pair's efforts to bring reconciliation to the two clans, and to persuade their respective chiefs to allow them to wed, the union was forbidden.

In despair, Lady Jane drowned herself, and ever since her ghost has haunted the castle. Her green gown has led to her being given the name of the Green Lady, and she is reported as being a most quiet, seemly, and attractive young woman, demure in dress and bearing but with a sad and lonely expression on her lovely face.

She is most often seen on sunlit evenings between five and six o'clock, drifting through the rooms and along the corridors of the castle – and she is a particularly well-mannered ghost, always opening and closing the doors of the rooms she passes through, endlessly wandering and unable to find peace...

Earlshall Castle

~

This beautiful, unspoiled mid-sixteenth century castle, near St Andrews, Fife, was once the home of Sir Andrew Bruce – called "Bloody Bruce" for his cruel and violent persecution of the Covenanters (members of the Scottish Presbyterian Church). As he trampled on the freedom of the worshipers in life, in death his ponderous, booted footsteps can be heard, forever ascending the castle's spiral staircase. Perhaps he is trying to climb to heaven, to beg forgiveness of those he tortured when he was alive . . .

Earlshall was occasionally visited by Mary, Queen of Scots, who went there for the hunt, and her room, preserved as in her lifetime, is haunted by the phantom of a little old lady whose ghostly frame leaves a depression in the bed as though a solid body had slept there! She is rumored to have been a servant, possibly lady's maid to the Queen.

Other strange things happen on the estate. Objects have been known to vanish through no earthly agency – and there is a particular spot in the grounds which dogs avidly avoid, something invisible to humans unnerves them.

Shadowy forms have been glimpsed when there is no living person present. But possibly the most frightening occurrence happened when a visitor stumbled on the stairs: she felt an invisible pair of hands catch her before she fell . . .

Sir Walter Scott

~

At the window of the dining room stands the figure of a silent, motionless man in nineteenth-century attire . . .

The gracious, castellated property known as Abbotsford House, on the banks of the Tweed at Melrose on the Borders, was the home of Sir Walter Scott for the last twenty years of his life. The novelist largely designed the house and he planted many of the trees on the estate.

In 1818, during alterations to the building, loud, sinister, "violent" noises were heard, and at their height George Bullock – the agent in charge of the modifications – died suddenly. Ever since, eerie noises sounding like something heavy being dragged along the floor have been heard by numerous people, including Scott himself before his death . . .

In 1826 his main publisher, Constable,

became bankrupt, and with them the printers and publishers with whom Scott had been a sleeping partner. The combined debts were in excess of one hundred thousand pounds sterling – an enormous sum in those days. A proud and noble-hearted man, Scott took upon himself the payment of the debt, refusing all offers of help and declaring –

"...this right hand shall work it all off."

He tried to do just that, until his continuous overwork resulted in a nervous breakdown. He died in 1832, on a bed near the window of the dining room of the house for which he had such affection, the debt still not quite cleared...

In fact, the outstanding amount was recovered from his estate after his death, but it may well be that the ghost of this great and honorable man still haunts the house, still yearning to complete the task he set himself...

The Headless Drummer
of Edinburgh Castle

~

Perched on the granite crag of Castle Rock, overlooking the gray granite city of Edinburgh, broods the somber gray bulk of Edinburgh Castle . . .

This sprawling, convoluted and very ancient place, dominates the skyline from almost every spot in the city. It was first used as a military outpost in the seventh century, but there was a building on the site even earlier (reputedly a retreat for Pictish princesses). Over the centuries it has been added to until it is now a warren of dungeons and winding corridors, with high-ceilinged halls and low barracks, chapel and yard, steep steps, heavy gates and turreted promenades.

The Castle seen crowned heads, nobles and would-be conquerors come and go through the centuries, and is now the scene of the yearly Edinburgh Tattoo, the climax of the world-famous Edinburgh Festival. It would be surprising indeed if such a place did not have its fair share of ghosts!

Over the years a wide variety of people – soldiers, employees, residents and visitors – have seen ghostly apparitions; in fact, it has been said that one such sighting caused a soldier on duty to collapse.

In general, sightings are kept very quiet, and the visitor has to rely on the atmosphere of the place. It is known that in 1093 Queen (later Saint) Margaret died here, after hearing of her beloved husband's death. During its long history there have of course been other noble deaths at the castle. But perhaps the most memorable phantom is that of a headless drummerboy, whose silent, drifting form appears at irregular intervals and in different places within the castle bounds . . .

The Noisy Ghosts of Inverary Castle

~

Whilst not particularly old – most of the building dates from the eighteenth century – Inverary Castle is a magnificent structure and a worthy seat for the Dukes of Argyll, the head of the Campbell Clan.

The Campbells have a long and colorful history: the Clan came to prominence in the fifteenth century and the family have been powerful ever since. The eighth Earl was the leader of the Covenanters (members of the Scottish Presbyterian Church), and was beheaded in 1661, while the eighth Duke, a distinguished statesman, married a daughter of Queen Victoria. Both Dr Samuel Johnson and Robert Burns have been entertained at the castle in times past.

A harper dressed in the Campbell tartan, believed to be the ghost of a man hanged at Inverary, appears before the death of a member of the family. Even when the phantom isn't present, ghostly harp music can sometimes be heard, echoing around the castle...

Sudden loud, inexplicable crashing noises are heard coming from an uncertain source – no one knows what they indicate, but they are not made by any living person.

But perhaps the most bizarre – certainly the least frequent – apparition is that of a column of soldiers from Cumberland's army, resplendent in their red uniforms and marching six abreast along the road to Dalmally! Lucky indeed is the ghosthunter who manages to see that spectacular manifestation...

In the Shadow of Arthur's Seat

~

At the opposite end of Edinburgh's Royal Mile from the great Castle sits Holyroodhouse Palace, a gracious and handsome building with an adjacent Abbey, which is now little more than a ruin. The imposing bulk of Arthur's Seat, an extinct volcano, forms an interesting contrast and fitting backdrop to the venerable site.

The Abbey was founded in 1128, and the Palace grew out of the Abbey's guest house, which over the centuries has assumed its current sedate guise. But behind its formal exterior lurk tales of passion and treachery.

In the latter half of the sixteenth century, when Mary, Queen of Scots was in residence, her Italian secretary, friend and (possibly) lover David Rizzio was murdered here. He was stabbed by each of the fifty-six court acquaintances of her husband, Lord

Darnley — apparently because Mary, on Rizzio's advice, had refused to allow Darnley any official part in her rulership.

Rizzio's body was left at the Queen's door all night, and the place where he died is marked by a large, indelible bloodstain. His ghostly footsteps have since been heard in the Long Chamber . . .

Not long after Rizzio's murder, Darnley himself was strangled to death: the murderer was never discovered, but Darnley's ghost is reputed to haunt his own rooms and Mary's bedchamber, unable to rest, perhaps, until the assassin's identity is known.

And lastly, a Lady in Gray hovers near the Queen's audience chamber. She is believed to be one of Mary's ladies-in-waiting, but her precise identity is not known. However, she seems as faithful in death as she was, presumably, in life . . .

The most haunted place in Scotland...

~

Magnificent Glamis Castle has been inhabited since the fifteenth century, and is famous as much for its numerous apparitions as for its royal associations!

In the latter half of the fifteenth century, the fourth Earl of Crawford, Lord Glamis and two chieftains were gambling. An argument started, and the players began cursing God – and then the Devil himself appeared and doomed them to play dice forever in the same room high in the Square Tower of the castle!

The rattle of dice, raised voices and the sound of heavy footsteps can still be heard coming from the room in the dead of night, and ever since this tower has been the focus of hauntings.

But strange noises have been heard in other parts of the castle – mysterious hammering, loud knocking sounds, the creaking of the door that never stays shut no matter what heavy objects are wedged against it.

And there are phantoms aplenty. There is a madman who walks on the roof on stormy nights, across a spot now known as "The Mad Earl's Walk." A sad and ghostly little black boy – thought to have been a page, maltreated and maybe left to die some hundred or so years ago – sits patiently outside one of the sitting rooms, still waiting to be summoned from his vigil. A tongueless woman frequently runs across the grounds, gesturing frantically at her bleeding mouth, and a bizarre, indistinct, skinny figure has been seen darting along the castle's drive . . .

From an upper window gazes a sad, pale lady, watching, perhaps, for a lover who never came. More frightening, however, is the fiery red figure of a Lady Glamis, burned as a witch in Edinburgh. The figure floats above the castle's clock tower.

Then, of course, there is the Monster of Glamis. Around 1800, legend has it, a loathsome child was born to be the heir, a child with no neck and tiny stumps for arms and legs, of little intelligence but possessed of an almost supernatural strength. A special room was constructed and the child was hidden away, his existence known to only the Earl, his heir, the family lawyer and the estate manager.

Tradition says the monster lived to be over one hundred and twenty years old, and although now dead, is bricked up somewhere within the walls, still overshadowing the family with ominous memories. Perhaps the little Gray Lady, who haunts the castle chapel, prays for the soul of the unfortunate child, and it may one day find peace . . .

The Mad Earl of Cullen House

~

Parties and social occasions at this ancient seat of the Seafield family are often graced – if it can be called that – by the ghostly figure of a regal-looking man . . .

James, the third Earl of Seafield, was known as "the Mad Earl" – it was said that while of unsound mind he murdered a close friend and then committed suicide from remorse. His ghost, restlessly walking the staircases and corridors with a slow and stately tread, was seen by innumerable people over the years; his favorite haunt being the library.

In the early 1980s the house was converted into separate private apartments, but the psychically inclined may still feel the sad, disconsolate presence of the sorrowing Earl.

Black Andrew

Lady visitors to the grand and stately Castle of Balnagown, ancient home of the Ross Clan in the Highlands, may find their days – and nights! – disturbed by the ghost of a powerful man with wicked eyes . . .

Andrew Munro, local laird during the sixteenth century, was a strong, heavily built man who, it would appear, badly abused his position of authority. Feared throughout the area, he was credited with an enormous number of rapes, murders and the most iniquitous and evil acts imaginable. "Black Andrew" doesn't really express his villainy, although it may give some indication of the darkness of his soul.

Eventually the chief of the Ross Clan, finally tiring of Black Andrew's barbarity, ensnared the evildoer, put a rope around his neck, and threw him out of an upper window of the castle. He gasped out his last breath hanging outside the window of a Red Corridor bedroom . . .

Dogs now refuse to walk beside this part of the building, and ever since his death, whenever a new lady visits the castle, Black Andrew stalks the corridor, fortunately now powerless to cause any harm – although he wouldn't see it that way!

There is another phantom associated with the castle, a young girl with green eyes and a wealth of coppery hair, who, from her regal clothing, is thought to be the ghost of a Scottish princess murdered in the castle. Unlike Black Andrew, she is said to be a sad and gentle ghost, whose presence is announced by the rustling of her silk dress.

Macbeth

~

1ST WITCH: "All hail, Macbeth! hail to thee,
  Thane of Glamis!"
2ND WITCH: "All hail, Macbeth! hail to thee,
  Thane of Cawdor!"
3RD WITCH: "All hail Macbeth! that shalt be
  king hereafter!"

(Act 1, Scene III)

Can it be mere coincidence that Shakespeare, writing in 1606, chose to make Macbeth the Thane (chief of a clan and custodian of the king's lands) of the two most haunted castles in Scotland?

The construction of Cawdor Castle, near Nairn in the Highlands, probably began in the latter half of the fourteenth century although the central tower is surrounded by Elizabethan buildings.

Apparently it has been haunted for most

of its history – numerous people reporting being aware of ghostly presences, seeing spectral figures, and feeling a supernaturally freezing cold in one particular room of the castle at various times.

There is also the ghost of a slender, lovely young woman with no hands, who appears to have been the daughter of one of the earls of Cawdor several hundred years ago: her father hacked off her hands as punishment for daring to fall in love with the son of a rival chieftain.

A fitting location indeed for a murderer's home! The "Scottish play," as Macbeth is invariably referred to by all connected with the theater (even to name the work by its title is reputed to invoke ill-fortune), is regarded as unlucky in the extreme. Performances are said to be invariably accompanied by a series of disasters, from personal accidents to fires to, on at least one occasion, death.

It has been said that the Witches Song has the power to raise evil. Whether this is true or not, it certainly has the power to raise the hair on the back of your neck!

" . . . For a charm of powerful trouble,
Like a hell-broth boil and bubble."
"Double, double toil and trouble;
Fire burn and cauldron bubble . . ."

The Ghostly Housekeeper
of Applebank Inn

～

There has been a hostelry at Larkhall, Lanarkshire, since at least 1714, although it's appearance has changed over the years.

The current inn is haunted by the specter of a Black Lady – said to be the ghost of a native woman brought back from India by Captain Henry McNeil, the one-time owner of Broomhill House, which used to stand adjacent to the inn. She disappeared in inexplicable circumstances – only later for her wraith to be seen in and around the inn by employees, visitors and local people.

Other phenomena accompany her appearances – a cash register opens by itself, and objects have been found moved. But strangest of all, when she is present, empty tables have been found ready laid for meals. A helpful ghost indeed!

The Haunted Aerodrome

~

Montrose Old Aerodrome, Tayside, is perhaps now best known as the home of a Museum Society, but at one time it was a working aerodrome, built before World War I.

It boasts three notable apparitions who appear from time to time and have been seen by both local people and visitors – a phantom aeroplane, the ghost of an airman (thought to be Lt Desmond Arthur who crashed at the airfield in 1913), and a World War II Royal Air Force officer.

The officer is reputed to have been an unpopular man who also crashed at the airfield in 1942. There is a legend that the crash that killed him was deliberately engineered, and that in his impotent fury he is unable to find rest, haunting the aerodrome ceaselessly . . .

Aleister Crowley –
Laird of Boleskine House

～

On the southern shore of mysterious Loch Ness broods a large, many-windowed, single-storey house . . .

Originally built by the Honorable Archibald Fraser in the eighteenth century on land obtained from the Church, the property was acquired at the beginning of the twentieth century by the Great Beast, Aleister Crowley – the self-proclaimed "wickedest man in the world."

It was at this house that Crowley first performed the Abra-Melin Ritual, a fifteenth-century ceremony designed, in the first instance, to establish contact with one's Guardian Angel, and secondly, to bring all of Hell's demonic hierarchy to swear allegiance to the magician performing the rite.

Crowley failed to contact the Angel, but, of course, the demons arrived on schedule . . .

The house filled with strange sounds, mysterious shapes and shadows, and the flickering silhouettes of devilish figures. Objects disappeared, only to reappear later in different places. The housekeeper vanished, and one of the laborers on the estate went mad and tried to kill the laird.

Even the butcher in the nearby village was affected: on receiving an invoice on which the names of two demons had been negligently written, he accidentally severed an artery and bled to death. The eerie atmosphere and inexplicable happenings are said to continue to this day.

The location of the house and the existence of an underground tunnel leading from the house to a graveyard where Crowley is said to have practiced ritual sacrifices both add to the mystique and reputation of the property. However this did not stop Jimmy

Page, former guitarist with the Led Zeppelin rock group, living in the property for nearly twenty years. Maybe having the interior redecorated with mystically inspired murals improved the atmosphere.

DOUR WISDOM

~

The Scots have long had a reputation for shrewdness and thrift – a reputation that has often been caricatured as cunning and miserliness!

In reality, the Scots are pragmatic and realistic about life in general, and have a wealth of sayings offering advice, consolation, and acute observations on the human condition . . .

When I did well, I heard it never;
When I did ill, I heard it ever.

~

Trust not a new friend nor an old enemy . . .

~

Oh, that some Power the gift would give us
To see ourselves as others see us!
It would from many a blunder free us
And foolish notion . . .
    Robert Burns, "To a Louse" (paraphrased)

~

He has wit at will,
That with an angry heart can hold him still.

~

It is a good tongue that says no ill,
And a better heart that thinks none.

Nae man speaks ill o' what he loves the most . . .

≈

Better an empty house than a bad tenant!

≈

Rich folk hae many friends . . .

≈

A fool may give a wise man counsel.

≈

'Tis good to begin well, but better to end well.

≈

Dinnae speak o' rope to a man whose father was hanged.

He that's scant o' breath shouldnae try to play the bagpipes!

~

He stumbles at straw and trips o'er daisies! (He finds difficulties only where he wants to.)

~

A man is weal or woe as he thinks himself so.

~

Better buy than borrow.

~

He that counts all costs will ne'er put plough in the earth.

~

It is a pain both to pay and pray.

'Tis no sin to sell dear,
But 'tis a grievous sin to give ill measure.

~

Want o' wit is worse than want o' wealth.

~

He that does you an ill turn will never forgive you.

~

Ill doers are ill deemers.

~

If a man deceive me once, shame on him:
If he deceive me twice, shame on me.

Traditional Magical Trees

~

Some trees are sacred to the Fey-Folk, and damaging one – or even worse, cutting one down – can lead to great misfortune.

Rowan – Mountain Ash – is the most important. It is beloved of the fairies, who will not harm anyone or anything within its protective aura. Luckiest of all was to have a rowan tree growing near the door to your house.

Elder is also a protective tree, and tea made from elderflowers is a traditional cold remedy – it is also good for toothache if held in the mouth for a few minutes, while an infusion from the berries eases neuralgia. Elderberry wine is an ideal accompaniment to the meal taken at the fall equinox, for luck and good health throughout the coming winter – but remember to leave a small bowl of wine outside the house for the Fey-Folk!

The Hazel is a very special tree, credited with divinatory powers: its twigs make the best divining rods for water. Hazel nuts are reputed to grant wisdom to those who eat them. Its wood is not to be used for commonplace purposes.

The graceful Willow and the Alder are much-loved by water spirits, especially those inhabiting healing wells and springs. Herbs carried in baskets made from willow taken from such a tree are said to prove beneficial to the infirm. Infusions of the bark are used to relieve pain and fever: willow bark was the original source of acetylsalicylic acid – now better known as aspirin.

Hawthorn trees are also sacred to the Fey-Folk, particularly if three grow close together, when they may mark the spot where fairy councils take place.

Even a small sprig stripped from an ancient, churchyard Yew can have a powerful magical effect. If, in the days of clan warfare, a Highland chief were to take such a bough, hold it in his left hand, and publicly denounce an opponent, then even if that enemy were present he would hear nothing of the imminent threat although everyone else could hear it plainly enough.

There's many a fair thing found false.

~

Quality wi'out quantity
Is little thought of – mair's the pity.

~

He that's ill to hisself will be good to nobody.

~

A hungersome man cannae listen to reason . . .

~

A shored tree stands lang.
(Threatened folk have amazing powers of endurance!)

Breathes there the man with soul so dead,
Who never to himself hath said,
This is my own, my native land!
Whose heart hath ne'er within him burn'd,
As home his footsteps he hath turn'd
From wandering on a foreign strand!
If such there breathe, go, mark him well!
For him no Minstrel raptures swell;
High though his titles, proud his name,
Boundless his wealth as wish can claim;
Despite those titles, power and pelf,
The wretch, concentred all in self,
Living, shall forfeit fair renown,
And, doubly dying, shall go down
To the vile dust, from whence he sprang,
Unwept, unhonour'd, and unsung.

Walter Scott, from
The Lay of the Last Minstrel, *canto VI, i.*

❧

It is not lost that a friend gets.

Twa things a man should ne'er be angry at;
What he can help, and what he cannae help.

~

Honesty may be dear bought,
But can never be an ill pennyworth.

~

Little intermeddling makes good friends.

~

Better a stranger for a friend
Than a friend become a stranger.

~

Beauty's muck when honour's lost . . .

Bloodthirsty Rivers

~

Over the course of centuries people have come to realize that certain rivers seem to claim victims with almost uncanny regularity.

The Dean, in Tayside, is a slow-running river but nevertheless is reckoned to take a human life every seven years.

The Till, a tributary of the Tweed, is another slow river but a traditional rhyme maintains an ominous patience belies its apparent calm –

> Tweed said to Till
> "What makes ye run sae still?"
> Till said to Tweed
> "Though ye run wi' speed
> And I run slow
> For every man that ye drown
> I drown two!"

The Tweed itself, flowing through the Borders, is a potent threat to life, taking one life every year.

A craftsman must hae clothes,
But truth gaes naked.

≈

A bonnie bride needs little dressin':
A wee horse needs little groomin'.

≈

Ne'er take a hammer tae break an egg
When ye can do it wi' the back o' a knife!

≈

A good tale is none the worse
For being told twice.

≈

Good will should be taken for part payment.

≈

We can live wi'out our friends,
But not wi'out our neighbors.

No man can play the fool so well
As the wise man.

～

Let the bell-wether break the snow.
(Tried leaders are best in emergencies.)

～

What may be done at any time
Will be done at no time.

～

Do the likeliest and hope the best.

～

He never lies but when the holly is green!

～

We never miss the water
Til the well runs dry.

Wealth makes wit waver.

~

Women and wine, game and deceit,
Make the wealth small and the wants great.

~

God help the poor,
For the rich can help themselves.

~

Death defies the doctor.

Moon Customs

~

Sowing and planting should always be done with the waxing moon, so that as she increases in size, she influences the crops to increase also.

Plowing and reaping are best done at the waning moon but wood for boats must never be cut at this time, as the craft may fall prey to storms and unexpected capsizings as the moon calls the craft down to the watery realm she commands . . .

~

Carry a lucky penny with you at all times. If you turn it over thrice when you first catch sight of the new crescent moon, your pockets will never be empty.

~

He that talks to hisself speaks tae a fool.

Seek your salve where you get your sore.

~

The day has eyes and the night has ears –
Sae be wary what ye do!

~

When wine sinks, words swim.

~

Wilful waste makes woeful want.

~

He's no' the berry
Nor yet the bush it growed on!
(There's something a little false about him!)

~

It's a shy cat that makes a proud mouse.

Ye'd dae little for God
If the devil were dead!

~

'Tis an ill bird that fouls his ain nest.

~

Better my friends think me fremmit
As fashious.
(Better my friends think me a stranger for
not living in their pockets, than troublesome
through visiting too often!)

~

A good name's sooner lost that won.

~

Kindle the candle at both ends
And 'twill soon be a-dyin' . . .

Give your tongue more holidays
Than your head!

~

They're strange friends
Who cannae be bothered . . .

~

We can shape our bairns' clothes –
But we cannae shape their fate,
Nae matter how hard we wish.

~

There's a flea in ma troosers!
(I'm in trouble!)

~

They complain o' want o' money –
But no', alas, o' want o' sense . . .

Raise nae more devils than ye can handle!

~

Nae crow gets whiter for washing itself.

~

Far fowls flaunt fair feathers.

~

Set a stout heart to a steep hill.

~

Be a friend to thyself,
And others will befriend thee.

~

Old proverbs speak the truth . . .

The Stone of Destiny ...

On St Andrews Day 1996, after seven hundred years, the Stone of Scone was finally returned to its rightful home ...

For four hundred years the Stone of Scone laid in the abbey church of Scone, until Edward I captured (many would say stole) it and took it back to England, where it was set in the Coronation Chair (built especially to hold it) in Westminster Abbey.

For centuries English kings and queens were crowned, seated on this throne. And for the same number of centuries the Scots seethed with anger that one of their ancient treasures had been taken from them.

Legend has it that this stone was the one upon which Jacob rested his head at Bethel when he had his famous dream of the angels climbing to and fro between heaven and earth, and hence it was imbued with divine power.

The Stone of Scone was reputed originally to have been taken from Spain into Ireland, and later moved to Scotland by King Fergus, to find it's first Scottish home in Dunstaffnage Castle. Later it was moved to Scone, where it remained until 1296: traditionally, the Scots would rule the place where it was set.

Scores of kings, both Scottish and English, celebrated their coronation with the Stone of Destiny beneath them.

If all this seems like a lot of fuss about what is basically a lump of rock, it may be wise to remember that such ancient, venerable stones carry within them enormous talismanic power, and, like the megaliths of Stonehenge and Callanish, represent mankind's striving for understanding, permanence, and greatness . . .

Acknowledgments

~

Thanks to Matt Herd, California, for American spellchecks and last-minute netsearching, and Jill Staniforth, Manchester, for remembering important dates . . .

And special thanks to Alistair Milnes, in Edinburgh, for information, details and useful websites – and for the urban myth that Greyfriar's Bobby only stayed at his master's grave for so long because the miserly corpse refused to let go of the little dog's leash . . . !